MW00438811

Moving

A Memoir of Education and Social Mobility

ANDY HARGREAVES

Foreword by Nicola Sturgeon

Solution Tree | Press
a division of Solution Tree

555 North Morton Street
Bloomington, IN 47404
800.733.6786 (toll free) / 812.336.7700
FAX: 812.336.7790

email: info@SolutionTree.com
SolutionTree.com

Printed in the United States of America

Library of Congress Cataloging-in-Publication Data

Names: Hargreaves, Andy, author.
Title: Moving : a memoir of education and social mobility / Andy Hargreaves.
Description: Bloomington, IN : Solution Tree Press, [2020] | Includes bibliographical references.
Identifiers: LCCN 2019047195 (print) | LCCN 2019047196 (ebook) |
ISBN 9781951075019 (hardcover) | ISBN 9781951075026 (ebook)
Subjects: LCSH: Hargreaves, Andy. | Hargreaves, Andy—Childhood and youth. | Educators—Great Britain—Biography. | Social mobility. | Working class—Education. | Poor children—Education. | Education—Social aspects.
Classification: LCC LA2375.G72 H37 2020 (print) | LCC LA2375.G72 (ebook) | DDC 306.43—dc23
LC record available at https://lccn.loc.gov/2019047195
LC ebook record available at https://lccn.loc.gov/2019047196

Solution Tree
Jeffrey C. Jones, CEO
Edmund M. Ackerman, President

Solution Tree Press
President and Publisher: Douglas M. Rife
Associate Publisher: Sarah Payne-Mills
Art Director: Rian Anderson
Managing Production Editor: Kendra Slayton
Production and Copy Editor: Rita Carlberg
Content Development Specialist: Amy Rubenstein
Text and Cover Designer: Kelsey Hergül
Editorial Assistant and Proofreader: Sarah Ludwig

For my family

Men make their own history, but they do not make it as they please; they do not make it under self-selected circumstances, but under circumstances existing already, given and transmitted from the past.

—Karl Marx

I've always found my way somehow . . .
By taking the long way around

—Dixie Chicks

Acknowledgments

All authors are indebted to others who have contributed to their work—colleagues, coauthors, students, editors, research participants, and more besides. A memoir, though, also has its own distinctive set of acknowledgments of people who have been part of the life that it records, and I would like to recognize them here.

I benefitted from sharing drafts of this book with others who have had lives like mine, or who, at least, can empathize with that kind of life. At the time of my writing this, three good friends were also writing autobiographies of one kind or another, and I am grateful for interchanges with Michael Fullan, Howard Gardner, and Steve Munby. My secondary school classmate and fellow Burnley Football Club fanatic Dave Edmundson helped me fill out my recollections of my days in secondary school. Ges Hartley, my former housemate and bandmate, brought back things from university life that I had completely forgotten. The governors of Spring Hill Community Primary School in Accrington, Lancashire, and the school's extraordinary former head teacher Stephanie Grimshaw shared old school records, class lists, and inspection reports that helped this memoir become more than a collection of memories in my own head. My great friend and colleague Dennis Shirley enabled me to see which aspects of this peculiarly British autobiography might require further explanation to a U.S. readership. My larger-than-life brother Peter not only put me straight on some aspects of family history but also gave me excellent intellectual feedback on various parts of the manuscript. Lucy Hargreaves, my daughter, undertook essential genealogical research on our family's history. My wife, Pauline, validated my efforts, corrected some of my writing errors, and wisely persuaded me to omit two sex scenes!

Mel Ainscow's invitation to me to write a foreword for his 2015 book, *Towards Self-Improving School Systems: Lessons From a City Challenge*, gave me a first opportunity to draw on and explore my own idiomatic connection back to our shared cultural background in northern England, and to do this within a scholarly context. Some of my expressions from that foreword reappear in this book.[1] The *Lancashire Telegraph* has kindly given me permission to draw on material I supplied for an extended feature that celebrated my mum and her life.[2] Additional text on the interaction between distinction and disgust in social-class relationships was first set out in my peer-reviewed article for the *International Journal of Leadership in Education*.[3] All other content appears in this book for the first time.

Ironically, in a café around the corner from Buckingham Palace, Lee Elliot Major was kind enough to engage me in conversation about the relationship between my memoir, his own upwardly mobile life, and his impressive body of research and writing on social mobility. By accident, Douglas Rife, publisher and president of Solution Tree International, and I discovered we were both writing family histories, and after we exchanged many comments back and forth, he unexpectedly offered to publish my book, thereby cementing my gratitude forever.

Publishing memoirs is a departure for Solution Tree as well as for me. It has required both of us to review editorial guidelines, and I truly appreciate the constructive turn our discussions took about content and style to take my contribution to this genre to the best standard we could achieve together. In particular, I would like to thank Rita Carlberg, production editor at Solution Tree, who worked closely with me and carefully through the manuscript at every point, helping me avoid weak arguments, ambiguous interpretations, and unsupported claims. She has undoubtedly played a significant role in making this a better, more fluent book than it might have been, and I am grateful to her and all her team for that. Kelly Rockhill, Solution Tree's assistant marketing program manager, gave valuable creative input on the design of the cover.

Table of Contents

About the Author

Andy Hargreaves, PhD, was born and grew up in Accrington, Lancashire, in England. He is an emeritus professor at Boston College and holds visiting or honorary professorships at the University of Ottawa, Hong Kong University, the University of Stavanger, and Swansea University. He is past president of the International Congress for School Effectiveness and Improvement and adviser in education to the first minister of Scotland, and from 2014 to 2018, he also advised the premier of Ontario. Dr. Hargreaves is cofounder and president of Atlantic Rim Collaboratory (ARC), a group of nations and their ministers and professional association leaders committed to broadly defined excellence, equity, well-being, inclusion, democracy, and human rights in professionally run systems.

Dr. Hargreaves has given keynote addresses in more than fifty countries, forty-seven U.S. states, and all Australian states and Canadian provinces. His more than thirty books have attracted multiple outstanding-writing awards, including the Grawemeyer Award in Education in 2015, the highest-value award in the field. Dr. Hargreaves is ranked in the top twenty scholars with the most influence on U.S. education policy debate. In 2015, Boston College gave him its Excellence in Teaching with Technology Award. He holds honorary doctorates from the Education University of Hong Kong and Uppsala University in Sweden. Previous books include *Uplifting Leadership: How Organizations, Teams, and Communities Raise Performance* with Alan Boyle and Alma Harris and *Collaborative Professionalism: When Teaching Together Means Learning for All* with Michael T. O'Connor.

To learn more about Dr. Hargreaves's work, visit www.andyhargreaves.com or follow @HargreavesBC on Twitter.

To book Andy Hargreaves for professional development related to this book, contact pd@SolutionTree.com.

Preface

La vida no es otra cosa que una excusa para encontrar la manera de vivirla.

Life is nothing but an excuse to find the best way to live it.

—Carlos Páez Vilaró

This book has been unlike any other I have written. It is, most obviously, about my childhood and education through to the end of university. But it has also been written for the chords it may strike amongst others who have had similar lives of their own or who have witnessed those lives amongst parents, partners, children, colleagues, and friends.

It could never have been written without the existence of the lives that it describes—the everyday and often invisible lives of ordinary citizens who drive our buses and taxis, make our clothes, fix our appliances, clean our homes, keep us safe, serve us in the local store, and look after our children. The book is meant to speak especially to all those who have made sacrifices, given things up, left behind homelands, or taken on extra jobs so that they or their children could have the best-possible chance in life.

It is also a call to members of the political, economic, and cultural elites to give other people's children the opportunities that they so eagerly want and assiduously ensure for their own—by willingly paying more taxes rather than less; by committing to the restitution of public education, public libraries, and public life; by choosing a good state school rather than an exclusive private education for their own children so they will get an opportunity to mix with a wider society; and by making a personal moral sacrifice to have a little bit less so that others who have a less favourable start might have a little bit more.

Through the lens of personal experience, the purpose of this narrative is to shed light on the phenomenon of social mobility. Social mobility has taken on growing importance in recent years as a way to try to deal with inequalities in society—not by providing restitution for low income or absence of wealth in working-class communities but by creating opportunities and pathways for children from working families to move up the income-and-wealth scale compared to their parents, over time, mainly through education.

The concept of social mobility was invented by Pitirim Sorokin in the 1920s. Sorokin experienced considerable social mobility in his own life. The son of a struggling travelling craftsman, he rose to be a professor of sociology at Saint Petersburg Imperial University. Because of his anticommunist views, Sorokin was arrested several times, sentenced to death at one point, and then eventually exiled to the United States, where he went on to establish the sociology department at Harvard University.[4]

Sorokin was fascinated by the existence of social stratification—the layering of social groups and their members in society by status, income, and wealth. In contrast to Marxist advocacy for proletarian revolution as a means to overthrow social-class inequality, Sorokin developed an interest in social mobility and especially what he called *vertical mobility* as a way to manage the existence of stratification through movement across the layers of income and status.

Sorokin understood *social mobility* as "any transition of an individual, social object or value . . . from one social position to another." *Vertical mobility*—which could be ascending or descending, social climbing or social sinking—concerned "relations involved in a transition of an individual . . . from one social stratum to another."[5] Sorokin applied the idea of vertical mobility to groups as well as to individuals—something that will be explored further towards the end of this book.

Ours is a world of increasing social immobility rather than the opposite. It is as if more of us are static, socially paralysed, unable to move. If we could knowingly prevent physical paralysis or deterioration amongst individuals and refused to do so, we would be callous in the extreme. It's now a great calling of our society to halt and reverse the paralysis of social immobility by reducing inequality and contributing more of our income and our lives to the greater public good. The book's final chapter, in fact, builds on my own narrative of social mobility to set out three possible scenarios for how the frequency and quality of social mobility might unfold for people in general. These scenarios are *meritocracy*, where perfect mobility that gives everyone their just desserts can create as many problems as it solves; a *new aristocracy*, where those who have been socially mobile in one generation use their newly gained privilege to prevent others' upward mobility and their own children's downward mobility in the next; and *economic democracy*, where greater equality reduces the need and pressure for social mobility.

This book is about moving up, moving away, and moving on in a society where this kind of movement is rarely easy. And it is about the emotionally complex and moving experience of social mobility that manifests itself in anxiety, pride, stress, estrangement, relief, and much more besides. Whether you have been socially mobile, aspire to help young people be mobile, or occupy a position in policy or society where you can create conditions that enable others to become mobile, I hope that this is a book that might move you to help others around you move too.

Foreword

By First Minister Nicola Sturgeon*

As the first minister of Scotland, I don't have a lot of time to myself, but when I do, I love to read. I find that reading relaxes me and helps with the stresses and strains of work. As such, I aim to have a pile of books to look forward to, including those that have been recommended to me by friends, colleagues, and, as with this book, the latest publication from authors whose work I admire.

I have had the pleasure of working with Professor Hargreaves since 2016, when I appointed him to my newly formed International Council of Education Advisers (ICEA). Andy is a leading member of the ICEA, and I have greatly valued hearing about, and learning from, his detailed and extensive knowledge and understanding of educational leadership and collaboration. He has spoken passionately about the importance of effective school leadership and how an empowered teaching profession will be the key to delivering excellence and equity in all of Scotland's schools.

Even before his appointment to the ICEA, Andy Hargreaves had long been recognized in Scotland as a leading educator. He received the Scottish government's Robert Owen Award in 2016 in recognition of both the significant international impact of his work and his contribution to inspiring educational improvement here in Scotland. In short, we consider ourselves fortunate to have access to the extensive experience and expertise that Andy provides. In our efforts to create a world-class education system, his advice and insight have proven to be an extremely powerful and trusted independent resource.

That is why I was delighted when Andy asked me to write this foreword to his memoir, particularly as he writes so powerfully about a subject close to my heart: the unique ability of education to transform lives and to provide every child and young person with the same opportunity to succeed.

It is still the case that children's circumstances—where they live and their family background—can have a disproportionate impact on their chances of success. That is why I have made excellence and equity in Scottish education the defining mission of my government.

Andy's book sets out clearly the difference that a good education has made to his life, taking him from a working-class childhood in Accrington to emeritus professor at Boston College, a period as president of the International Congress for School Effectiveness and Improvement, and educational adviser to my own government. However, what really makes this book stand out is that Andy can look at education not only from the point of view of someone who benefitted from a first-class education but also as a teacher who worked in a range of schools and saw first-hand the impact that poverty can have on educational attainment. This understanding of the impact of poverty is strongest when speaking about his early teaching experiences in socially disadvantaged areas:

> *Being a good teacher was no longer a matter of making learning interesting or boring, of succeeding or failing at the job. It was now a matter of making a difference to children who were on the wrong end of class inequality, and this was something I now felt driven to do.*

His growing realization that there is more to teaching than enabling children to pass exams, and the importance of educating the whole child, is clearly established in chapter 7, where Andy is "confronting a more deep-rooted approach to teaching and learning and the curriculum in schools that suited students from privileged families more than those whose parents or guardians were economically impoverished or culturally marginalized."

However, the point at which this book began truly to resonate with me is at the beginning of chapter 3, when Andy begins to discuss his education and says, "Beyond playing outside, though, my biggest memories were of school. Teachers must be careful what they do with their students. The memories of it can last a lifetime." The absolutely crucial role that good teachers can play in the life of every child is something that I too recognize, as someone who has also experienced the kind of social mobility that Andy describes throughout his book. I believe that young people have the right to a first-class education, and the most fundamental element of that is ensuring that we have an outstanding and empowered teaching profession. That is why Andy's work as a leading educator and proponent of educational improvement is so important.

The book's message to me, as a political leader, is that "social mobility is too important to be left to individual effort, ingenuity, luck, or chance. Systems and governments must play their part as well."

CHAPTER 1

Move On Up

Such a boy is between two worlds of school and home; and they meet at few points.

—Richard Hoggart

I'm going to a university award ceremony at the top of a hill to receive first prize in a national competition. I'm not the only person who's going. Many cars, shiny black classic ones, are heading up there in front of me. Looking down, I realize I'm not in the same kind of vehicle as theirs. I'm lying on my stomach, arms out in front of me, pulling my car and myself up the hill with my hands. It's incredibly hard work. I look up. The other cars are getting away from me. So I pull harder, dragging myself forward, knuckles bleeding. Suddenly, I feel a surge of power in my arms. Improbably, I start to catch up. Then I overtake them. When I reach the summit, I'm the first to arrive.

It's surreal. Literally. Then, the dream—for that's what it is—turns into a back-and-forth composite of two scenes. In one, I'm surrounded by ethereal academics—Oxbridge and Harvard types—in an oak-beamed room. They're asking me pointed questions about esoteric aspects of art, literature, and history. One shows me the parchment of a classic poem written by a famous ancestor of his, with barely discernible words in Latin, that he presumes I can interpret. I'm mystified by this and by other questions from his colleagues, and I clumsily bluff my way through them, acutely aware that he and the others may catch me out at any moment. These donnish scholars assume and almost insist I must already know all the answers to the competition I won, that it was all part of the cultured person I'm supposed to be. But they don't know I looked up all the answers, spending hour after hour, day after day, deliberately memorizing what they imagined I should already have possessed. I succeeded illegitimately, it seems, and any moment now, someone will find out and my award will be null and void.

Meanwhile, in a parallel scene, a distinguished school superintendent on the selection committee is peering over his spectacles and sounding off about impractical education professors, their heads in the clouds, with no understanding of how to operate in schools in the real world. Somehow, I sense, these derisory remarks are directed at me and others like me. In this scene, I'll get my award, but it won't be deserved or worth anything to those I'm supposed to serve in the field.

This isn't a fictional dream. When I was putting the final touches to this book, it's one that woke me up, sweating, in the middle of the night. It doesn't take a doctorate in psychoanalysis to interpret it. It's about the experience of social mobility. Like Curtis Mayfield's 1970 lyrics about the African American community that urges them to "move on up toward your destination, though you may find from time to time complications," it's a dream about a kind of progress that doesn't come without personal struggle—without, in Mayfield's words, having to "keep on pushing."[6]

As many women, African Americans, impoverished immigrants, and people who come up from the working class know only too well, moving on up means pulling twice as hard with half as much as most of the others around you to make any kind of progress at all.

And then, when you get there, wherever it is, even at the very top, there remains a feeling that you still may never be fully accepted or truly belong.

Narratives of Mobility

What happens to people who, against considerable odds, do reach the top? How do they experience, express, and explain their success? Somehow, as in my own case, others may convey a distinct feeling that the rewards are not merited, that they have been achieved by fraudulent means, and that all of us who have received them are impostors whose shabby secret of sheer hard work is about to be revealed at any moment.

Sometimes, those who are upwardly mobile will internalize these messages and feel, as I can be inclined to do, that being invited onto some austere panel of distinguished minds has only happened because someone else wasn't available, or has died, or didn't fit some odd category (the token Brit on a U.S. roster, perhaps) they may happen to represent. In my own case, for example, after the vice president of Scandinavia's oldest university, Uppsala, called to inform me I was being awarded an honorary doctorate, and explained that previous recipients included Jane Goodall, David Attenborough, and Nelson Mandela, I spent the next week checking out whether an old mate of mine had got a friend of his to put on a Swedish accent to play a practical joke on me!

Other people can and do respond to social mobility differently. They may adopt the defiant stance of Canadian rap star Drake, who sings, "Started from the bottom, now my whole team f——ing here." Having come from a modest upbringing, Drake gets the irony of it all. "Now I'm on the road," he snarls, "half a million for a show."[7] Conversely, those who are socially mobile can abandon the values of their upbringing and fully internalize those of the elites they have joined, feeling only pity or contempt for those they left behind. Or they can take up causes and become champions for their gender or race or the class they were born into.

Social mobility has many narratives—narratives of dreams and struggle, of alienation and insecurity, and of deal-with-it defiance. American memoirs of social mobility tend to be heroic, up-by-the-bootstraps stories of surviving poverty, chaos, and even outright abuse to reach the pinnacles of achievement and acceptance. British narratives are more ambivalent and angst ridden. They are more typically about being caught uneasily between two cultures and not properly belonging to one or the other. If the British-born part of me starts to articulate the stresses and strains involved in being upwardly mobile, my U.S. friends retort, "But, Andy, don't you see? You're the complete embodiment of the American Dream!"

Some people, including me, actually experience a maelstrom of multiple narratives of what to do and who to be that involves a whole range of more and less noble emotions at one time or another—the humility of remembering where we came from alternating with guilty relief about our own success; defiance in the face of obstacles and authorities one minute and cringeworthy anxiety at a gathering of elites the next; outrage when the class or culture of our origins is insulted or ignored by intellectual and political elites, alongside frustration with the racial intolerance and xenophobia that persist amongst pro-Brexit relatives and lifelong friends. In Curtis Mayfield's words, where social mobility is concerned, from time to time, there are definitely complications.

Part of these complications is that mobility doesn't walk alone. Its pursuit of equality and equality of opportunity isn't undertaken in isolation. Social mobility has two stalwart companions. One is the struggle for acceptance, identity, and belonging amongst people who move from one culture to another. It's about fraternity or sorority. The other is the pursuit of liberty—the quest for freedom, autonomy, and dignity against unbending institutions and unwarranted authority that block the efforts to be mobile or to achieve self-realization. Sometimes these things run together, like a modern re-enactment of the French Revolution. Liberty, fraternity, and equal opportunity! At other times, like in the 1960s' British student counterculture, freedom in the face of authority can fly off at an anarchic tangent, without much concern for social-class equality and mobility or even for any abiding sense of community and belonging.

These are the many ways that social mobility can play out, then—leading to moral struggles for greater equality, libertarian pursuits of freedom, or drives to achieve success as acts of vindication or even revenge against the elites who try to hold people back. But this book is not, primarily, an academic analysis of social mobility. It is a window into the phenomenon of social mobility that hinges on my own personal experience of it. It documents how social mobility has affected and still affects me, especially through education, and it connects this personal narrative of opportunity and identity to the issues and major research studies of the past and of the present day.

A lot of the book is grounded in my own lived experience. The book claims to be no better or worse than those of others who have written about their own experiences of mobility. Journalist Lynsey Hanley had to strive to succeed while growing up in the 1980s on a vast Midlands council estate in England.[8] Distinguished education professor and former teacher Diane Reay was the eldest of eight children from a mining family on another Midlands council estate in the 1960s.[9] Novelist Jeanette Winterson was raised in the same small mill town of Accrington as me, by strict religious fundamentalists.[10] Darren McGarvey somehow survived alcoholism, substance abuse, and homelessness to escape from the poverty of the Glasgow Gorbals in the 1990s and become a prominent advocate for poor families everywhere.[11] Bestselling U.S. author J. D. Vance grew up and away from the hillbillies of Appalachia and Ohio to go to Yale and beyond.[12] And Tara Westover completed a doctorate at Cambridge University in the United Kingdom after escaping the clutches of her strict and sometimes violent family of Mormon scrap-metal dealers in Idaho.[13]

We share similarities of class but also differences of gender, generation, country, upbringing, and much more besides. Yet, one way or another, these are all still stories of mobility, identity, and liberty. They are part of what Hanley recounts from the 1950s' writings of U.K. cultural theorist Richard Hoggart as being an experience of moving up, up, and away, emotionally as well as physically, with every certificate gained and hurdle overcome.[14]

Then there are others, of course, who are less endearing to the literati, who didn't take up causes, fight against injustices, or become the individualistic and lost literary souls who appeal to modern-day social scientists, quality journalists, and top-notch educators. But self-made business entrepreneurs who started with nothing and achieved everything themselves have undergone social mobility too. They are the likes of Duncan Bannatyne, multimillionaire health-club and property entrepreneur and former star of the U.K. TV series *Dragons' Den* (the forerunner of the U.S. *Shark Tank*). He only got going when he bought an ice-cream van at the age of thirty, following a Glasgow childhood raised with six families in one house and a dishonourable discharge from the navy for throwing an officer overboard. Bannatyne's heroic business narrative and self-help motto is the title of his first autobiography, *Anyone Can Do It: My Story*.[15] As a self-proclaimed, self-made, street-fighting man, Bannatyne probably wouldn't have much sympathy for what might strike him as self-indulgent whining amongst an oversensitive bunch of upwardly mobile milquetoasts.

My own narrative is meant to add to this collection and to the genre as a whole. It draws on my own and other people's memories, family stories, genealogical details, and official records from my old schools, to connect my own lived experiences to the experiences that others were undergoing at the same time, as they were recorded in key studies and intellectual arguments of the day. In this sense, the book is about me and others both like and unlike me in the working-class communities of Northwest England. (For readers who don't come from my part of the world, it is important to point out that this is why the book is written not only with British spellings but also in the idiomatic language and occasional dialect of the community that raised me.) It is also about a moment when there was more social mobility than at any other time in modern history, before or since.[16]

The book is also about how the educational issues arising from and impacting on social mobility still retain importance for so many people. They encompass:

- The ways people deal with leaving one culture to join another
- The nature and effects of early selection by tested ability
- The impact of high-stakes testing on students from disadvantaged homes
- The strengths and weaknesses of whole-child education as a way to engage working-class and minority students with educational opportunity
- The consequences of some young people becoming socially mobile while their neighbours or siblings are left behind
- The question of whether attention deficit hyperactivity disorder (ADHD) is a distraction that needs intervention or an expression of creativity that challenges traditional methods of classroom control

This is a memoir about the public systems that create or hinder opportunity, as well as a personal narrative of benefitting and not benefitting from that opportunity. It is about public investment, personal struggle, social class, educational reform, and, here and there, little bits of luck as well.

What's Worth Writing For

For a long time, I thought my life was not worth writing about. In fact, I didn't even consider writing or not writing about it as an issue. I've spent a lot of my career writing about other people's lives—mainly in schools and workplaces—but I didn't feel I was much to write home about myself. I'm not a celebrity chef, athlete, politician, rock musician, or reality-TV star. I don't come from royalty, I have an unspectacular ancestry, and I never had a life or a job where I hung around the rich and famous.

At the same time, I'm not a rags-to-riches person, a competitor for Frank McCourt's *Angela's Ashes*,[17] or somebody who—in Monty Python's terms—was born in a shoebox and was glad of it![18] I'm not a recovering addict, a lottery winner who won it all and then lost it, or a survivor of some immense personal tragedy. All these lives are well worth reading about. But they are not my life, my unremarkable life, a life that was never worth keeping a journal for, because who would possibly be interested in it? In the working-class culture I grew up in, we thought of ourselves as nothing special. We had dignity and self-respect, of course, but we didn't feel we had any standout features that could put us on a pedestal above anyone else.

But the older we get, and the more we learn about other people in our families, communities, and workplaces, the more it becomes evident that we are all remarkable in some way or other. All our lives have themes that connect us with the lives of others—love and loss, triumph and tragedy, weddings and funerals, hope and disappointment, leaving home and coming back. It is these points of connection between our stories and other people's stories that establish points of interest. Sometimes, it's not one person's story over another that is at issue. In the words of the 1970s working-class comedian Frank Carson, stories are like jokes. What matters is "the way we tell 'em."[19]

The moment I truly grasped all this was when my mum was dying in Accrington Victoria Hospital in Lancashire, England. She was ninety-three years old. Because of unbearably painful conditions and what had become a dismally poor quality of life, she had decided to take no further nourishment. After she lapsed into apparent unconsciousness, my family and I sat with her for the best part of nine days until her final breath. I thought the time would pass slowly, but the hands raced around the clock at the end of her bed. Over many hours and days, I wrote a short piece about her life—the stories she told, the experiences she had, the things she did—at first, just for its own sake, and because, as a writer, I knew it was one of the few things I could usefully do.

The narrative took on a shape, and I sent it off to the *Lancashire Telegraph* that my mum used to have delivered every day—a widely read daily newspaper across one of the most populated counties in England. I submitted it not as an obituary but as a tribute to my mum and also to a way of life shared by women like her and families like ours throughout the region.

The editor wrote back, asked for some photographs (which we had luckily already collected for Mum's ninetieth birthday, her last big bash), and announced they would publish it as a major feature. Just a couple of days before Mum died, when all the fluid had practically gone from her body, I leaned right over her with family members gathered around. I had no idea whether she could still hear.

"Mum," I said, "I've something to tell you. I've written a piece about you for the *Lancashire Telegraph*. They say they are going to publish it as a double-page spread complete with pictures. It's all about you and your life, Mum. A double-page spread! Here's how it starts."

I turned to my text. "Here's the headline"—the one the editors had assigned to it—"How a Loving Accrington Mum Scrimped and Worked for Her Family."[20]

And then I began, "Doris Hargreaves was born in a commode at the back of a sweet shop in Accrington, two years after the end of the Great War . . ."[21]

Barely two sentences in, something happened that we thought was no longer physically possible. From the corner of my mum's eye, out of a tiny frame that had received no fluid in over a week, a single tear fell slowly down her cheek. Then I stopped. She understood. She knew. And so did I. This life, these lives—lives like ours—are absolutely worth writing about, as many people appreciated when they wrote back to me about the piece in the weeks that followed.

After the editor asked me questions about what this brief biography meant, they published my remarks at the beginning of the article. I wrote:

> *The point is not that my mum had an especially extraordinary life; but that she gave meaning to the underrated virtue of sacrifice.*
>
> *She cared for others throughout her life by how hard she worked and what she gave up for them.*
>
> *My mum's working class life also perhaps expresses something about the social history of the town and the region, as well as its people.*[22]

This is basically a story about what many members of my parents' generation thought they were giving up some of their own lives for. But it's not a simple narrative of sacrifice and reward, of investment and return. It's about what happens to us when we move up, out, and on. It's about what changes and what stays the same in the contours of our lives and in what Martin Luther King Jr. famously called the content of our character.[23]

Step by Step

Across the span of almost seven decades, I've made what feels like a huge change. I've moved from a two-up, two-down rented terraced house with no indoor toilet, on a cobbled street, in an old Victorian mill town, to being a reasonably well-known (some would even say quite famous) professor, writer, speaker, and government adviser in my field of education. These days, almost every month, I meet with a minister, president, ambassador, or other dignitary, at his or her request. I've lived and worked in three countries and, with my family, become a citizen of two. That's a lot of movement.

But big changes in life circumstances usually come through smaller increments, the many tiny steps that define social mobility. This book covers the first two decades of my life with my family, in my community, and at school and university, and it is about these less grandiose but equally important changes. It is about moving in the mid-1950s, with the support of the welfare state, up the hill on the back of a coal truck and into public housing—and then, with a bit of good fortune, into a small owner-occupied terraced home. It's about moving up from infant school—known in North America as kindergarten and first grade—to junior school, from being with the whole range of children in my neighbourhood to just the ones who were selected for the A stream. It's about moving on, to join the 15–20 per cent or so of my age group who went to grammar school, and travelling across town to get there, from one side to the other. It's about walking there and back, a mile each way, four times a day (though not uphill both ways!), with an ever-shrinking group of fellow students who stayed on beyond the minimum leaving age. Then it's about moving away, off to university, as many like me did, and never truly going back.

Social mobility lifts some people up. Others are left out or get left behind. They include my two brothers, who didn't pass the test that would have got them to grammar school and who therefore weren't allowed to learn the things they wanted—history, art, music, and sport. Rather than going to university on the other side of the country, they ended up in factories at the bottom of the hill. The left-behind also include the kids who were down in the primary school B stream, who went to secondary modern or vocational schools, who left school early and mostly worked in their overalls while we went to school in our uniforms. They were also the kids who picked out and picked on the "snobs" and the "swots" like me, who had been arbitrarily elevated above them from the age of seven, with insults and fights—breaking my brother's violin and giving me a black eye for my trouble. Social mobility is a process of exclusion as well as inclusion. At the same moment some are able to step up, others discover they are falling more and more steps behind.

Leave or Remain

So once you move up and out from your class and community, what is it that changes about you, and what stays the same? When you come home from university, or a plum job in a new city, or back from another country altogether, do your family and friends rejoice in saying, "You haven't changed a bit!"? Or do you let it all go to your head and put your past behind you? How do you reach for the stars yet keep your feet planted firmly on the ground?

Uruguay's superstar football player—*soccer player* in U.S. terms—Edinson Cavani puts it this way. In a letter to his nine-year-old self, Cavani tells him he will fulfil his dreams of making lots of money, driving nice cars, and sleeping in fancy hotels.[24] But the constant travel will take its toll, he warns, and he will not always be happy. So he urges his younger self to always remember:

> *You live your life outside, with a ball at your feet. This is the way in South America. You don't know anything different. What's inside, anyway? Nothing fun. Nothing interesting. No Playstation. No big television. You don't even have a hot shower. There's no heat. . . . When you want to have a bath, you get a water jug and heat it up over the kerosene stove.*[25]

Cavani insists that wherever he's playing in the future—a vast stadium, a big cup final—his younger self should always find a way to "feel the dirt under [his] bare feet."[26]

There's no dirt under the feet for me, even though, in my childhood, I did have my baths in a metal tub in front of the coal fire. But there was and is the millstone grit on the peat-bog moors, high above the chimney tops of my upbringing. The grit is what I walked across, mile after mile, with my big brother after my dad had died. It's what our stone terraced houses and the cobblestones of our streets were fashioned from. It's what my playmates and I knelt on in our short pants when we rolled coloured glass marbles and steel ball bearings down stone slabs in the schoolyard. And, if you're lucky, it's what remains in your character that becomes part of the landscape of your soul wherever you find yourself in the future. This is not just Angela Duckworth's grit—the grit of sheer perseverance or tenacity in response to daily adversity.[27] It's also the grit of defiance in the face of obstructive and oppressive authority.

As you move up, on, and out, you hope you hang on to some of these things. You hope you'll continue to stand up to and stand with others against injustice and exclusion. Despite all your travels across different countries and cultures, you hope that when you open your mouth, people will still be able to tell where you come from. You hope you'll retain some of your interests and TV-viewing habits, however unsophisticated and unfashionable they may be amongst the intellectual elite. You hope you'll remember to treat all people with respect and dignity and acknowledge their humanity by thanking and conversing with them—the driver who lets you off the bus, the waiting staff at a conference dinner who never get noticed or receive any tips, and the people cleaning the toilets in the train station or the airport—because you remember how your mum used to clean people's houses and how, when your own children were small and you were struggling financially, your wife was a waitress in the local pub and sold Avon cosmetics door-to-door in the evening. You also hope you do all this simply because it's the decent thing to do.

But you also know you are moving in different circles now. Your accent will change a bit as you go from place to place. The subjects of the conversation will shift and widen—and why shouldn't they, for don't these worlds of literature or opera or international travel open your mind to other people's perspectives? Isn't this what your education was for? After all, one Latin root of *education* is from *educere*, meaning "to lead out." But you'll also feel uneasy when comfortable elites are smug or patronizing, when they search for a weak spot in your knowledge, your manners, or your bearing so they can put you back in your place.

Will you rebel? Will you stand up for yourself and others who are being slighted? Will you hold your tongue to keep the peace? Or will you respond with rapier-like flashes of cutting wit? Perhaps, like Drake, you'll accomplish even more success just to show *them* a thing or two at thousands of dollars a show. Sometimes, like former U.S. ice skater Tonya Harding, when the judging is stacked against you because you like to do the equivalent of skating to rock and roll, not to orchestral classics, you also know you'll just have to pull off your own unanswerable equivalent of a triple axel so they can't, for shame, hold you back any more.[28] Whatever the question, you'll ultimately have to answer with your work.

But what will you say when you go back home and the family you love makes racist remarks or sexist jokes? What will you do then? Who will you be? How will you take advantage of every opportunity that has come to you, including that of an open mind, yet also keep the ball at your feet and the grit between your teeth?

There'll be no balanced life for you—not for many years, at least—for this aspiration belongs only to the privileged. They already have something to balance. You'll work relentlessly hard, knowing that on the ladder of upward mobility the rungs beneath you never stop falling away.

Social mobility is neither unambiguously heroic nor inescapably tragic. The path of social mobility, the process of moving on up, has complications—for everybody. This book is about my own path and the paths of others. If you are mobile, have been mobile, aspire to be mobile, or can influence others in their own efforts to be mobile, it's a book that might have something to say to you.

CHAPTER 2

No One Likes Us; We Don't Care

And this is the place where our folks came to work
Where they struggled in puddles, they hurt in the dirt

—Tony Walsh

"It's coming! It's coming!"

May Kenyon was sitting on the commode at the back of a sweet-shop, or candy store, in the small mill town of Accrington in Lancashire, England.

"Don't be daft, May. It can't be," said her mum.

But May's mum was wrong, and out popped my own mum, Doris. Doris came from the womb of May in the month of May. It was 1920, just two years after the end of the Great War. Beginnings do not get much humbler than this. For what would become the Hargreaves family, the only way now was up.

The first child in her family, and the only girl, Doris was named after a nurse who'd saved the life of Doris's father, William Kenyon, during the flu pandemic that had swept across Europe when the gassed and wounded returned from the trenches.[29]

Bill was my grandma's second cousin. On her side of the family tree, there are one or two trunks where branches should be! The marriage choices for women in Accrington at the end of World War I were sparse. Seven years younger than my grandma, half-deaf as a result of bombshell damage, and congested in his lungs all his life because of mustard gas poisoning (and a habit of chain-smoking Woodbine cigarettes), Bill was one of the town's lucky soldiers who had returned from the war alive and relatively intact.

Doris and Albert

When Doris wasn't at school, in the back of her family's two-up, two-down terraced house, she would care for her younger brothers, Raymond and Stanley, and wash the tins and trays her mother would need for the tiny bakery she ran out of their front room. The Depression forced the family to close the bakery. These were hard times for many. Doris even recalled having to take a pram to the local pit to scavenge slack, or bits of coal, for the downstairs fire.[30]

Doris left school when she was fourteen and, for a few shillings a week, went to work in weaving, munitions, and carpet-sweeper factories. In one of her jobs, she had to twist wire coils by hand, which caused her palms to bleed. She protested and was subsequently given her cards. She arrived at the employment exchange to find that her former supervisor had called ahead, recommending they not give her work because she'd been fired for insubordination. Later in life, Doris often recalled having "prayed each day for that factory to burn down." Uncannily, a few months after she'd been let go, it did![31]

Doris was not averse to a good time. In her old age, she sometimes spoke wistfully about a dashing airman she would go to dances with at the seaside in Blackpool, where her mum's relatives still lived. As a teenager, she carried a torch for her cousin Lesley, who died when he crashed his motorcycle. Doris kept Lesley's memory alive by choosing his name as the middle name for her firstborn son, Peter.

In an uncompromising working-class culture, my brother did not thank her for burdening him with what was widely regarded as a girl's name at the time.

From time to time, Doris would also enjoy a good night out with her glamorous cousin and lifelong best friend, Vida, until her dad put a stop to this when she came home late one night—by ripping her dress from her shoulders and throwing it on the fire.

Doris was a strong and independent woman. As a teenager, she could dive off the top board in the public swimming baths. She could still do cartwheels into her sixties. Even in her nineties, she refused to the last to walk with a stick and preferred "furniture walking" instead! She had wanted to be a nurse and was desperate to be a Land Girl—going away from home to live and work on the farms while the men were at war. But her class and her father wouldn't allow it. So, as many women like her did, she put her strength and sense of service into her family, her housework, and her friends instead.

During World War II, Doris married Albert Hargreaves at very short notice, when he received his papers for posting to Egypt (though, at the last minute, flat feet spared him from probable death, and he was posted to British coastal defences instead).[32] Albert was seven years older and seemed reliable and steady. But my mum's father still disapproved of them getting married and was convinced that my dad's papers were forged. He stubbornly refused to come to the wedding until the very last minute—something he repeated with his youngest son, Raymond, many years later. Doris fought her dad to marry my dad, and, as in many of her other life's battles, she prevailed.

Albert was the youngest son of a clogger—a maker of wooden clogs for the local mill workers. He was supporting his mother, by then a widow, who, with an arm mangled by factory machinery, lived on a disability allowance. Albert's mum was heartbroken when she heard he was going to get married. She had imagined he would look after her for the rest of her life. Albert was quiet and calm. A dispensing chemist, or pharmacist, with a grammar school education, and good with numbers, he rose quickly to become a sergeant major in the Royal Artillery.[33]

Doris gave birth to her three boys—Peter, Colin, and then me—all three years apart and first raised us in a rented terraced house round the corner from her mum. A few years ago, our old street gained notoriety when the local council took Brendan Rodgers, Liverpool Football Club's former manager, to court for allegedly failing to maintain and repair a property he owned and rented out there. The case was dropped when the council didn't file its paperwork in time![34]

Though wartime was over, rationing and austerity were still realities, so life didn't get much easier. The front-room floor was a threadbare carpet square spread across green linoleum. The stone-paved kitchen was separated from the front room by an old army blanket our dad had brought home when he was demobbed, or demobilized, from the military—the earliest memory from my childhood. For my mum—and all the town's working-class women like her—maintaining a clean home was a constant struggle. For all but two weeks a year, when most families left for their annual holidays, the factory furnaces and the coal fires in people's homes kept the town under a thick pall of smoke and ash.[35]

By the mid-1950s, Britain's postwar welfare state brought benefits to our family as it did to many others. We may only have been able to afford to move house on the back of the coalman's lorry, but going up to the council estate where my mum and dad had been offered a home gave us a bath, a garden, and privet hedges.[36]

Typical of many postwar parents, Doris and Albert wanted to ensure their children had opportunities. School uniforms and caps were always spick and span. My older brothers went across town for violin lessons. And the annual holiday to the seaside by steam train was the treat for which Doris saved up all year—a week in Southport, three holidays in a row in Fleetwood, and, most exotically, even one overseas trip to the Isle of Man. Mum wouldn't buy this on tick, or credit. "If you can't pay for it, you shouldn't have it," she'd always say. She often worked two or three jobs—childminding, cleaning, and shop work—to acquire those extras and make ends meet.[37]

Many of these habits and values have stayed with me all my life. Work hard. Don't expect things to come easily. Seize your opportunities. Make sacrifices. Never get into debt. Value a good education. Persist. But, whatever happens, always take and enjoy your holidays.

Northern Grit and Wit

When we grow up, most of us are shaped by our families, of course, but also by the language, landscape, and culture of our classes and communities. Accrington is in the northwestern part of England, a region around Manchester, described by Prime Minister Benjamin Disraeli in 1838 as "the workshop of the world."[38] Barely a mile away from our house, James Hargreaves (no traceable ancestral connection) invented the spinning jenny—an innovation for rapidly winding fibre that revolutionized the cotton industry by replacing weavers with machines. Indeed, so revolutionary was Hargreaves's invention that it brought a visit from a gang of Luddites, who placed a hammer in his hand and forced him to destroy his own technology.[39]

Accrington is a small former textile town of around forty thousand people in ranks of slate-roofed terraced houses that march up the hillsides to the moors. On my way to secondary school, I used to walk past hundreds of factory workers, standing outside in their navy-blue boiler suits, drinking hot tea from their pint pots on their union-required tea break. In its heyday, the town was booming.

The mills and the engineering factories are all gone now. So, too, are the Nori brickworks (*Nori* is *iron* in reverse) that, amongst other things, provided the foundations for the Empire State Building in New York and for Blackpool Tower—England's diminutive facsimile of Paris's La Tour Eiffel.[40]

Accrington's singular and somewhat dubious claim to national fame is its football team. Accrington was one of the twelve clubs that founded the English Football League in 1888, the first such league in the world. In 1962, it was also the first club to be expelled from the league because of bankruptcy (it eventually reformed in 1968 and re-entered the football league in 2006, where it sat in the bottom division until its improbable promotion to the division above in 2018). I vividly remember my dad taking me to games as a child, where he stood me on top of an upturned brass shoebox so I could see. I might not have been raised *in* a shoebox, but once a fortnight, I was raised *up* by one!

In the 1980s, the club's misfortunes were parodied in a TV advertisement for the Milk Marketing Board. It shows a boy being teased by his friend, who says that the then famous Liverpool Football Club striker Ian Rush told him that if he didn't drink all his milk, he would only be good enough to play for Accrington Stanley. "Accrington Stanley? Who are *they*?" the boy asks. "Exactly" is his friend's riposte![41]

Accrington is a subject of national derision, an old musical hall joke, a place that nobody ever goes to without a very good reason. In 2018, *Express*, the digital extension of the right-wing tabloid *Daily Express,* judged it to be the eighth-worst town in England (amongst a list of ten that mainly consisted of other towns from the Northwest).[42] Even Mum said that the only good thing about Accrington was that you could get out of it easily.

"Leave as soon as you can," she used to say to us boys. "There's nothing here for you." She probably overstated her case because, eventually, one by one, we all did leave—for Canada.

In their own way, though, the people of Accrington were, and still are, fiercely proud, warm, and welcoming. The Northwest is built on forthright men and feisty women whose families once worked in the ear-splitting atmospheres of engineering factories and weaving sheds. My mother, grandmother, uncles, and brothers all had jobs there at one time or another. A few hours spent on Ancestry.com reveals no hidden British aristocracy in our family tree. The only alleged claim to fame is that of Kenneth Wolstenholme, the TV commentator for England's victory over Germany in the 1966 FIFA World Cup Final and creator of that memorable phrase that accompanied England's final goal, "They think it's all over. It is now!" He was reputedly the distant cousin of my grandma, whose maiden name was Wolstenholme too.[43]

Going back several generations, a scan of family occupations brings up *weaver*, *weaver*, *weaver*, with repetitive regularity. The noise of the weaving sheds was deafening. In secondary school, at the end of the school day, I used to visit my brother Colin's velvet mill, where he repaired the looms. Our conversations were conducted in improvised sign language amidst a lung-scouring fog of white cotton fluff. After years of doing this kind of work, my grandma became a quick and skilled user of official sign language when a deaf couple moved in as her next-door neighbours. There's a reason we all still shout sometimes, men and women alike, why we sound like foghorns, especially after a few drinks. It also explains why many of us talk with our hands and wave our arms about—something that has stayed with me as an ineradicably eccentric part of my public-speaking style.

In Accrington and the Northwest generally, people's voices are loud. Their style is direct. They have no side, or pretentiousness, to them. They speak as they find. Like female Manchester TV detectives Scott and Bailey (the 21st century northern-English reinvention of America's Cagney and Lacey), they are bold as brass and matter of fact.[44] They know how to bear up when things are hard and laugh raucously at themselves and each other when they cock things up. Modesty is not a quiet expression of pious humility. It's about bringing each other down a peg or two when the moment requires it, about not getting too big for your boots, and about genuinely applauding each other's triumphs as well. If ever I got to be top of the class or did well in an exam, my granddad would joke, "We'll have to widen t'door so tha' can get tha's 'ead through!"

Living rooms, pub lounges, market stalls, football terraces, corporation buses, and backyards where the washing was being pegged out—all of them were places of endless bantering, gossiping, joking, and piss-taking; complaining about menfolk and womenfolk, officialdom, and authority; and cataloguing of a vast assortment of ailments, including, amongst middle-aged women, mysterious conditions "down there!" Talk would overlap; mild swearing such as "daft bugger," "bloody hell," and, later, "stupid wanker"—but never the f-word—was mandatory; and broad Lancashire dialect prevailed.

"If thah wants summat doin', tha mun do it thissen" ("if you want something doing, you should do it yourself"), my mum would often say. "Earning a wage" was "gerrin summat aggled," in my grandad's words. "Something or nothing" was "summat and nowt." And if someone was "agait this and agait that," he or she would be "doing one thing then another." Most of the thick dialect has gone now, but strong accents remain and are even making a bit of a comeback. These days, "the internet" is "t'internet"! When you walk down the streets of Accrington, or get on one of its buses, you'll still be greeted with "Alreet" or "Hiya" by practically anyone you meet.

Grit, determination, courage in the face of adversity, and scant respect for the repressed emotionality and southern affectations of elite English authority were and still are core characteristics of

Northwest cultural life. Northwesterners are collectively proud of their efforts and industry but also feel that, like anyone else, they are really "nothing special."

This working-class childhood and adolescence of the 1950s through the mid-1960s, it needs to be said, was, in racial terms, almost completely white. Immigrants from Pakistan who came to work in the town's cotton mills didn't arrive in large numbers until I was reaching the end of secondary school. There was no visible diversity at all in my primary school. At grammar school, the diversity extended only to the four or five Jewish boys who mysteriously disappeared before our daily morning prayers and returned just as mysteriously afterwards.

Underneath the railway viaduct was the town's only Indian restaurant, where young working-class men, like my eldest brother, tested their virility with excoriating vindaloo curries after a few beers on a Friday or Saturday night. The lone Chinese takeaway was the only other local opportunity for any culinary diversity. Apart from these exceptions, Accrington and the towns around it were almost completely white working class, through and through.

A harbinger of what was to come, though, occurred in a local workingmen's club that made national news. Accrington's Old Band Club was the last workingmen's club in England to impose a "colour bar," voting by a two-thirds majority in 1964 to exclude an applicant who was a Sikh. Commenting on the judgement, the club's president stated that the "time is not ripe for social intercourse between ourselves and the coloured people."[45] I'd like to think my dad, who had been one of its members, had he still been alive, would have voted to oppose this ruling, but, of course, we'll never know. Although traditional northerners were and are deeply loyal to their own historic communities, they could show themselves to be deeply mistrustful of newcomers and outsiders—a pattern that has persisted right up to the days of Brexit Britain.

In general, traditional northerners love being underdogs and are defiant in the face of condescension and petty bureaucracy. Six miles to the north of Accrington is Burnley. It's the smallest town ever to enter the English Premier League of football. The entire population of Burnley can easily fit into the stadium for Manchester United. Burnley Football Club got to the Premier League and has played in its upper reaches, just below Chelsea and the like, with prudent local ownership rather than the lavish expenditure of overseas investors. When I interviewed former chairman Barry Kilby for a book I coauthored, *Uplifting Leadership*, he pointed out that Burnley constantly "punches above its weight." It relies a lot on local investment and community pride. He smiled at the thought of overseas billionaires from the United States, Russia, or the Middle East, who have no such long-standing loyalties and "have to get out a route map" to locate the club they are buying. "I can't bet the ranch" on overseas playing stars, he said, and risk plunging the club into debt.[46]

So Burnley takes journeymen players that other clubs have discarded, or faces that haven't fit; selects them on the basis of a strong work ethic; and forms them into an organized team. The resulting play is rarely easy on the eye. There are few flashes of creative brilliance. And on "Match of the Day" TV highlights, Burnley performances often come on last, after the glamorous big-city clubs, and receive only the most grudging praise for the team's dour efforts. But the chant of the crowd at Burnley's matches epitomizes the defiance of the town's population more generally:

We are Burnley, super Burnley.
We are Burnley, from the North.
No one likes us. No one likes us. No one likes us.
We don't care.

This could just as easily be a chant for Brexit Britain (Burnley, which voted 67 per cent in favour of leaving Europe in the 2016 referendum, was selected by the BBC as one of the most pro-Brexit towns in the nation).[47] It could also be an anthem for Trump supporters in the former manufacturing towns of the United States and for the Ford Nation voters (named after Premier Doug Ford) in Ontario, Canada. Indeed, it could be the theme tune of the white working class and lower-middle class in many countries who have come to feel ignored by political and intellectual elites or treated by them as objects of derision and figures of fun.

Distinction and Disgust

The wit and grit of English northerners is not the kind of England that populates the American imagination. The country that gave the world the language of Shakespeare, that founded the ancient universities of Oxford and Cambridge, and that transmits the plum vowels of the BBC World Service across the globe appears to many to be the international epitome of cultured learning and good manners.

Impressions of England's elite accomplishments emanate from the bits of England that have been selectively portrayed in classical literature, modern film, and televised costume drama. This is the England of the pastoral South: of *Pride and Prejudice*, *Vanity Fair*, and other period drama and of anything involving the posh pronunciations of privately educated, multisyllabic actors like Benedict Cumberbatch and Helena Bonham Carter!

But there are other Englands—working-class Englands, Asian Englands and Afro-Englands, and manufacturing Englands—ones that Americans rarely see. These are also often ignored, abandoned, or belittled by the upper-middle classes and southeastern elites of England itself. Until recently, the only place where people from the Northwest appeared on public media was in comedy or as villains, peasants, and fools—unless, like actor Sir Ian McKellen (otherwise known as Gandalf) from Burnley and nearby Bolton, they had almost lost their northern accents altogether. Only in the past few years have we started to hear strong northwestern accents amongst TV newsreaders. And a remarkable thing about the long-running British science-fiction series *Doctor Who* is not just that, for the first time, Doctor Who is a woman, played by Jodie Whittaker, but that, out of thirteen Doctor Whos over time, she is one of only two to possess a strong northern accent.[48] The other is Christopher Eccleston. Eccleston, who has also appeared in a number of U.S. movies and TV series, like *The Leftovers*, was raised in a working-class family in Salford, now part of what's called Greater Manchester.[49]

Not so many years ago, at an international conference, I had to take a colleague aside who was from the Home Counties around London. At this and other conferences, the first greeting to my wife and me was usually in a parody of a northern accent—"Eeh by gum. Ecky thump! Ello luv!" My colleague didn't mean any harm, of course, and is a good friend to this day. But in England, I responded, a couple of years before Brexit and Trump, why were the northern white working class in this person's and others' comments still fair game as the last acceptable prejudice of middle-class intellectuals and elites?[50]

In classical literature, apart from the windswept romance of Emily Brontë on the blasted heaths of *Wuthering Heights*, northern England has been either neglected altogether or portrayed as a grime-ridden world of pitiable monotony. This is how Charles Dickens depicted the Lancashire town of Preston, near to where my wife, Pauline, and her family come from, when he visited it in 1854:

> *It was a town of red brick, or of brick that would have been red if the smoke and ashes had allowed it; but, as matters stood it was a town of unnatural red and black like the painted face of a savage. It was a town of machinery and tall chimneys, out of which interminable serpents of smoke trailed themselves for ever and ever, and never got uncoiled. . . . It contained several large streets all very like one another . . . inhabited by people equally like one another, who all went in and out at the same hours, with the same sound upon the pavements, to do the same*

> *work, and to whom every day was the same as yesterday and tomorrow, and every year the counterpart of the last and the next. . . . You saw nothing . . . but what was severely workful.*[51]

In the Depression of the 1930s, privately educated George Orwell indulged his acquired socialism by spending several weeks in the lodging houses of Northwest England to write *The Road to Wigan Pier.*[52] With graphic depictions of working-class poverty in settings such as tripe shops and mining communities, Orwell had what one of his biographers, Thomas Ricks, described as an olfactory obsession.[53] Compared to his own fortunate distinction, the working classes, like the "natives" of the Indian subcontinent where Orwell started his colonial career, were disgusting. They stank.

Socially successful individuals often have either inherited or acquired what the late French sociologist Pierre Bourdieu termed *distinction*—the "pure taste" that enables a person to see him- or herself as separate, or distinct, and able to determine what should be refused or avoided.[54] In his book *The Theory of Moral Sentiments*, Adam Smith—better known as the author of *The Wealth of Nations*—explained and approved of this sense of taste:

> *It is the acute and delicate discernment of the man of taste, who distinguishes the minute, and scarce perceptible differences of beauty and deformity . . . who excites our admiration, and seems to deserve our applause; and upon this foundation is grounded the greater part of the praise which is bestowed upon what are called the intellectual virtues.*[55]

Wherever they are on the political spectrum, those who have distinction set the very standards of disgust, deciding what people should reject or find repulsive: "the tawdry, the cheap, the fulsome."[56]

Those who are socially unsuccessful, or fail to possess distinction, can then turn into the objects of others' disgust. According to Charles Darwin, in *The Expression of the Emotions in Man and Animals*, *disgust* "refers to something revolting, primarily in relation to the sense of taste as actually perceived or vividly imagined."[57] In its simplest sense, Darwin observed, *disgust* means "offensive to the taste."[58] Disgust is an elementary as well as an alimentary emotion. It makes the nose turn up and the lip curl.[59]

Disgust is also a moral emotion, as Darwin himself acknowledged when he commented how disgusted he felt when he was in Tierra del Fuego and "a native" touched his food. People and objects can be the source of our disgust. And in our reactions to people who disgust us, "we seem thus to say to the despised person that he smells *offensively*" [italics added for emphasis].[60] People disgust us not only when they are grotesque but when their actions seem vulgar or cheap, when they fail to possess discernment and appear to embody all that is indelicate and obscene.[61]

Disgust and distinction, then, are the emotions of social exclusion—the means by which people may shrink from those who are disabled or express contempt for those whose race, ethnicity, or social class is different from their own.[62]

Distinction recoils when presented with expressive emotionality, labelling it as *gauche* or *trash*. Those few of us who somehow manage to achieve social mobility while hanging on to our own emotionality often report feeling out of place in our education and our lives. Profound depictions of this dilemma can be found in *Strangers in Paradise*, a collection of autobiographies of people from working-class backgrounds who went on to teach and work in the university setting. These narratives reveal that no matter what these individuals achieve, or how successful they become, even when they are presidents or vice chancellors of universities, they still feel like imposters who don't belong.[63] Often, this is because of their language; their "vulgar" speech, as others interpret it; their emotionality and direct manner of communication; and their lack of restrained humility, which, they find, embarrasses, offends, or disgusts their colleagues.[64]

I am definitely amongst them. For more than fifteen years, Boston College has been extremely supportive of me. I could scarcely have asked for more, and I remain one of its biggest supporters. But one thing I have never got the hang of is quiet humility. If you are congratulated on your achievements, what you are supposed to say is "It wasn't me, really; it was all the others." Most do say something like this. Many even mean it. Where I grew up, however, humility was a tool of oppression to keep the accomplishments and aspirations of the poor down. We were proud of what we could do against the odds. We were underdogs. We were not deferential. We were defiant. We celebrated every victory against authority, adversity, and exclusion. We trumpeted our own and one another's achievements gloriously. It's one thing to choose poverty or humility. It's another thing altogether to have it thrust upon you.

My northern exposure has given me a lot professionally. It's made me outwardly animated and inwardly grounded. It's affected my habits and my hobbies of engaging in popular culture, which often help me establish a connection with teachers—many of whom also came up from the working class. But it's also put me at a distance, sometimes, from my colleagues in the academy. Take TV as an example. I have good friends and colleagues in U.S. universities who will watch little else than American public broadcast TV that is viewed by around only 2 per cent of the U.S. population. There are other academics who proudly possess no TV at all. I can and do watch the costume dramas and intellectually oriented programmes of my academic peers, but especially when I am travelling and doing a bit of casual hotel viewing, I will, without a shred of guilt or irony, also watch many things that are part of popular culture—*Deadliest Catch*, *Ice Road Truckers*, *Strictly Come Dancing*, *The Bachelor*, *Naked and Afraid*, *The Amazing Race*, *Eurovision Song Contest*, anything with Bear Grylls, and all kinds of sitcoms. I do draw the line at *Keeping Up With the Kardashians*, however (even though I once found myself with Kim Kardashian in a casino elevator in Australia!). I love karaoke and a chance to belt out "Sympathy for the Devil" or "Total Eclipse of the Heart"! On a good night, I bowl better than 160, and I can usually hold my own in a game of pool in almost any bar in town (though it has nearly got me into trouble on more than one occasion).

I love these things about popular culture not because I am curious about them from an anthropological distance or because I somehow think I should be but because I genuinely enjoy them. My wife calls it my Blackpool gene. Blackpool is the coastal town where my grandma and her magnificently named sisters, Primrose and Bertha, grew up. It is now one of the poorest towns in England (also fifth on the *Express*'s worst-towns list), a casualty of easily available air travel and cheap foreign holidays.[65] It is and was a town of funfairs and gambling, of bawdy postcards and silly hats saying "Kiss Me Quick." It's where we used to visit our endlessly talkative auntie Vera and my illiterate and innumerate uncle Ted (who nonetheless had a successful business installing fireplaces that his wife did the accounts for). Their loud teenage daughters ran around their council house in their over-the-top outfits, the TV was always blaring in the background, and uproarious laughter, as well as repeated brews of hot tea, reminded us always that we were very welcome. Take me back home, and I'll talk to anybody and everybody on the bus, at the football game, or in the pub. I sometimes ask my wife to wear a bit more bling than she has on, even though I know I really shouldn't, and then I quickly apologize, claiming it was my Blackpool gene that made me do it.

Oddly, all of this helps me connect with educators, with my students, and in workshops and lectures around the world. After a few public spats about targets and testing, I sang "You've Lost That Lovin' Feelin'" to my colleague and old friend Michael Fullan in a debate in Toronto in front of more than a thousand school principals from all over the world (something he writes about in his own autobiography too!).[66] Many years ago now, I received positive workshop evaluations from head teachers back in Lancashire saying, "I really liked the swearing." After my family and I had become Canadian citizens in the 1990s, I even did a fake striptease in front of a hundred school principals and my visiting mother-in-law to reveal a T-shirt saying "My Canada includes the Hargreaves" (this turned out to be the only thing I ever did to improve my relationship with my mother-in-law).

Some of this is theatre, of course (we will see more of this later), but some is also what I grew up with—being quick on your feet, emotionally direct, and brutally honest; being prepared to stand up for yourself and for others who can't; kowtowing to no one; telling it like it is; connecting to everyday life; being a bit irreverent or even utterly shameless sometimes; and, as John Lennon once put it in an interview with the Beatles, just "havin' a laugh."[67] My humour that can be an asset in my presentations has a bit of Monty Python about it but also, like Sir Ken Robinson—if not quite so brilliantly—a touch of the end of Morecambe Pier, a place where in the 1950s and early 1960s comedians would perform for working-class families during their seaside summer holidays.

There are times when I look at the strange skill set I have and rejoice in my Blackpool gene. But the very things that can enamour me to my classes and audiences at home and abroad can, however, also sometimes alienate me from colleagues who express and experience their emotions differently than I. This is my failing as much as theirs. Like the lyrics of an old Everly Brothers song, sometimes people think I "talk too much" and "laugh too loud."[68] In meetings amongst American colleagues, my staccato voice with its northern vowels can sound to me and to them like an interruption and an intrusion, so I sometimes end up contributing less rather than more than I really should. American norms of middle-class conversation, at dinner or elsewhere, are to ask a question, receive a considered response, and politely wait your turn while listening to the next person. Northern-English banter, like French conversation, or chatter between twins, though, is to talk over people, overlap, make a comment, and interrupt, not because you're not interested but because you are. This can come across as rude or just mansplaining in the United States, but where I come from, the women, including my wife's formidable sisters, do this as much as or even more than the men.

So now you know a bit about my family and community and the origins of my specious way of being. There'll be more about them later. But for now, it's time to go to school.

CHAPTER 3

How the Light Gets In

Childhood is measured out by sounds and smells
and sights,
Before the dark hour of reason grows.

—John Betjeman

You don't see children playing out much unsupervised these days. You also don't see drivers without seat belts, diners smoking inside restaurants, and teachers going out for lunch and a pint of beer on Fridays before they return to their classes either. So we have to beware of romanticizing the past.

But the truth is, we did play out a lot, and there was nobody to organize us except ourselves. We played football, cricket, and hide-and-seek at night by the lamppost on the street corner. We poked bits of tar between the cobblestones with sticks and collected old cigarette packets and brightly coloured beer-bottle tops from the gutters as our own kind of treasure. Occasionally and mischievously, we also knocked on people's doors and then ran away. None of this would be acceptable today, of course.

Beyond playing outside, though, my biggest memories were of school. Teachers must be careful what they do with their students. The memories of it can last a lifetime.

Spring Hill and Its Streams

Spring Hill Primary School was in an 1899 stone building, a monument to the start of mass public education, a half-mile walk from home every morning, down the cinder-covered backstreets. There were no buses, cars, or school runs. Most of us walked to school by ourselves, taking in a few puddles along the way and, once we got home, getting scolded for ruining our lace-up shoes.

The infant school, for children ages five through seven, was in a separate, smaller building, a bit further down the hill. Eileen Whittaker was its kind, matronly headmistress. A few weeks before going up to the juniors, at age seven, I was called up to Mrs. Whittaker's desk at the front of the class, where she gave me, like the students before and after me, a vocabulary test. The words were easy at first and then got progressively more difficult. I received effusive praise when I successfully struggled through the phonetics and even the meaning of *pneumonia*. Then, after two or three failed attempts to pronounce *phthisis*, the test abruptly came to an end. (Isn't it interesting how, for the rest of our lives, we can often recall these moments when we failed a test more easily than we can the times when we passed one?) Why on earth somebody devised a test item that expected a seven-year-old, even a linguistically precocious one, to pronounce a word meaning "pulmonary tuberculosis or a similar progressive wasting disease," straight after *pneumonia*, defies the imagination even to this day.[69]

What I didn't appreciate at the time was that this test, along with Mrs. Whittaker's other information and judgements about me, were being used to determine the kind of primary education I would get for the next four years—and probably the kind of life I would have after that. Half of the seven-year-olds, along with me, would go into the junior school A stream, or A class, where we would first encounter the kindly older-sister figure Miss Pope. She was followed by the reality shock of a woman in fierce horn-rimmed glasses who would shake me and anyone else senseless in front of the whole class for merely talking out of turn. The somewhat austere Miss Sutcliffe in year 3 seemed not so bad after this, and as we shall see, the inspired teaching of Miss Hindle in the top juniors, for ten- and eleven-year-olds, was nothing short of an educational revelation that had a profound influence on the rest of my life.

The other half went into the B stream and got a different set of teachers, culminating in the school's only male teacher, in 4B (the lower stream in the top juniors), a stocky bald man with a built-up shoe on one leg—the result, perhaps, of a war injury or a lifelong disability. We never knew.

I don't recall being prejudiced about people with disabilities. For instance, a young man in his twenties at the bottom of our street had severe cerebral palsy. Although his limbs seemed to be at war with his mind, and his speech was almost unintelligible sometimes, we marvelled at the ingenious contraptions he invented for playing hands of cards and performing other everyday tasks. I also counted a girl with spina bifida amongst my best friends. This included our shared role in the school Nativity play where we each played half of God, issuing eerie commandments in two-toned unison from behind the vaulting box in the school hall. I was the back half—or God's bottom, to be precise!

But if you have a disability or even a small physical curiosity and you attract dislike for any other reason, often it's the "deformity" that gets the attention. The dislike in this teacher's case stemmed from the way he handled discipline. Those of us in the A stream class came across him when all the boys from 4A and 4B would do craft while the girls did sewing. For me, this was a class to dread, not just because of my habitual disorganization that would leave me with bits of paper and smudges of glue all over my face and clothes but also because the teacher seemed to take perverse satisfaction in belting boys with his rubber slipper for the slightest infraction.

In the A class, we were lucky; we had him only once a week. The B class was condemned to get him most of the time.

Decades later, for reasons that will become clear later in the book, the governors of Spring Hill shared some old class lists with me. On one side were the names of my peers and me divided into two different streams at age seven—one list for the boys, another for the girls. On the other side was the name of the school each student went to after he or she took the selection test at age eleven and moved on to secondary education.

The eleven-plus, as it was known, determined whether students would go on to grammar school and the high probability of university after that or on to secondary modern school (the British equivalent of vocational school) and a likely future in manual work instead. Most of the students—twenty-eight of them—in the A stream went on to the boys' grammar school or the girls' high school. When I read through the list, many of the names in that A stream were still familiar—I'd walked home with those children, gone round to their houses sometimes, played with them in the schoolyard or out in the woods, sung with them in concerts, or collaborated with them on projects.

I could recall almost none of those whose names were listed in the B stream. I'd never met the children except for the little hard lad who'd picked fights with many of us—including me.

Years after junior school, when I was in my twenties, I'd found myself on a Sunday lunchtime in a greasy-spoon café at Accrington Bus Station. A short man with broken teeth called to me across the counter.

"Andy! Andy!" he shouted. "It's me!"

At first, I didn't really hear him or realize he was addressing me. So he called out again.

"What've you been doing?" he asked.

I was a doctoral student by this time, but because doctoral study was a rarity then, I mentioned that I'd been in teaching, as this seemed to be a more easily understood point of connection.

"What've *you* been doing?" I inquired in return.

"Three years. Strangeways Prison. Robbing gas meters," he answered.

Luckily, he hadn't been aware it had been my brother, by then a policeman, who had arrested him.

By and large, from the age of seven, streaming kept students from middle-class or *respectable* working-class families apart from the *rougher* elements of the working class—as sociologists, for decades, had classified those within this group.[70] We were already living separate lives, building different networks, going down divergent paths. No students allocated to the B stream went on to grammar or high school. They all ended up in secondary modern schools instead. (By this time, around 1960, the technical school, like many others across the country, had been consolidated into a secondary modern.) As the Jesuits said, when they cited the Greek philosopher Aristotle, "Give me a child until he is seven, and I will show you the man."[71]

A Child at Seven

Spring Hill's streaming policy was not unusual. One of the first and most important studies in educational research in the United Kingdom examined the life courses and opportunities of a cohort of more than five thousand British children born in the first week in March in 1946. By 1954, these children were eight years old and had typically already spent a year in streamed classes, as I would do four years later. What effect would streaming at age seven have on them by the time they went on to secondary school at age eleven? This was one of the key questions asked by Professor James W. B. Douglas, the principal investigator of this landmark study, in his classic 1964 book, *The Home and the School*.[72]

Just under five hundred children in the Douglas study went to two-stream primary schools, like mine. One of the conventional wisdoms of the time was that streaming reflected natural ability, even if this correlated with social class. Put students of similar ability together, it was argued, and teaching them would be more effective. And if there was a mistake in the initial selection, or if some students proved to be late bloomers, it was always possible to make adjustments later on.

To many educators at the time, opposition to this view seemed far-fetched. When, in the early 1960s, northern sociologist Brian Jackson asked teachers who supported streaming to characterize their opponents, they came up with views that destreaming was supported by "teachers who find non-streaming a useful gimmick" to get them promotion, "teachers who care more about starting new fashions than the welfare of children," "earnest reformers who are disposed to accept slogans and emotionalism," "ivory-towered lecturers in education," and "sociologists with no practical experience."[73]

These judgements aren't specific to their time. In the late 1980s, I provided evidence to a parliamentary select committee in Ontario, Canada, related to the province's practice of streaming in grade 9. A couple of years later, I coauthored a government-funded report that was associated with the abolition of streamed classes at that age.[74] In response, within a couple of days of each other, I received two letters. One accused me of being a fascist. The other, in threatening prose, ominously printed in big letters cut and glued from a newspaper, alleged I was a communist.

But despite all the entrenched opinions about streaming and destreaming, then and now, the gaps between streamed classes in the 1960s widened; there was little mobility between them; and the more the pace of instruction and expectations were adjusted to each stream, the harder it became to move from one to the other. Douglas's study showed that between the ages of eight and eleven, the test scores of students in the A streams improved while those of students in the B streams actually deteriorated. The achievement gap between students in the A streams and B streams widened, and only 2 per cent of students per year transferred upwards.[75]

Streaming reinforced initial differences—ones that were also strongly associated with social class. I was lucky. I made it into the A stream and then on to grammar school, university, and beyond. Others were far less fortunate, and their very different futures had been set out before them when they were just seven years old.

ITV's long-running, highly successful *Up* series put some wrinkles in this pattern.[76] In 1964, it decided to follow a sample of twenty seven-year-olds from a carefully selected range of social backgrounds. When one of three boys in a private preparatory school announced that he liked to read the *Financial Times* to see how his stocks and shares were doing, and when a tough working-class boy was filmed being a bit of a rogue on the adventure playground, it seemed highly predictable that there would be a class society in the making. Indeed, the opening commentary foretold how "the shop steward and the executive of the year 2000 are now seven years old."[77]

But as Michael Apted, the second director of the series, returned to interview the initial subjects every seven years into adolescence, adulthood, and the start of old age, the initial fascination with the perpetuation of social-class differences through education gave way to delving into the often surprising and sometimes gripping personal life stories of individuals' human development.

One of the three privately educated schoolboys, for example, undertook missionary work overseas and taught in a challenging London comprehensive school. The little working-class ruffian who wanted to be a jockey ended up becoming a London taxi driver and eventually bought a second home for his wife and family in Spain. The introverted farm boy from the Yorkshire Dales in the North of England emigrated to America to become a physics professor in Wisconsin. And every seven years, viewers were desperate to find out what would become of Neil, the promising and optimistic middle-class schoolboy who aspired to be a coach driver and wanted, as I once did, to take people on holiday tours. Heartbreakingly, Neil turned into a morose adolescent, then a depressed squatter in abandoned properties, then a tenant with obvious mental-health problems, who lived a squalid life in a caravan in the rainy North of Scotland. Eventually, and miraculously, though, he successfully ran for office as a local politician. Education, this series seemed to be saying, wasn't really about class destiny after all. It was about unique individual life stories.

But nobody from the elite end of the sample of seven-year-olds fell all the way to the bottom. And nobody who began at the bottom rose all the way to the top. The attention of the series itself also had a halo effect as subjects became more reflective about their own lives, and Neil was able, in part, to turn his life around because of the kindness and support of the former missionary.

Streaming still undermines mobility. In 2013, the Organisation for Economic Co-operation and Development (OECD), which compares the educational achievements of more than seventy of the world's most developed economies, found that "in countries and economies that sort students into different education programmes at an early age, the impact of students' socio-economic status on their performance is stronger than in systems that select and group students later."[78] So deciding to employ the simple strategy of delaying streaming until age fifteen and beyond can still carry a significant benefit for students from disadvantaged backgrounds.

From my point of view, in 1958, at the age of seven, being selected into the A stream was definitely a stroke of luck—though not completely of chance. This was not my only benign twist of fate.

Our Stroke of Luck

In 1960, our family had its own stroke of luck. Mum wasn't finding life easy, and on one memorable day, many things had gone wrong. They culminated in her knocking over a bottle of milk on the doorstep she'd just cleaned. Northern-English working-class women scrubbed their stone steps every week, lest they be thought dirty and slovenly by their neighbours. It was a way that *respectable* working-class families separated themselves from *the roughs*.[79] Therefore, to Doris, this accident was a stain on her character, as well as a puddle on the step.

When Dad came up the garden path from work, Mum let rip as only she could. The children had been naughty. There'd been an argument with a neighbour. Then the milk bottle went over. It was too much. After each recounted incident, my dad, the steadier one in the family, stood there calmly and asked, "Have you finished yet?"

When my mum got to the milk bottle, he put his hand on her shoulder. "Sit down," he said.

She did. He handed her an envelope.

"What's this?"

"Go on. Read it," he urged.

The letter was from a Sunday tabloid newspaper. It announced that my dad had won 500 pounds (over 10,000 pounds in current value) in a newspaper competition by placing the top-twelve reasons for cleaning your teeth in the correct order and by penning a caption superior to everyone else's.

After being raised in the Depression, getting married in wartime, and bringing up her family through years of austerity on the edge of poverty, Mum had great difficulty imagining anything good could ever happen to her. "Well, it must be a trick," she said.

But Dad insisted it was true, and it was. So Doris and Albert bought a small terraced house on a cobblestone street for 650 pounds with a deposit from the winnings.[80] The house had no bathroom, central heating, or indoor toilet, but it was ours, and whatever else happened, our mum insisted, prophetically, we would "always have bricks and mortar over our heads."

I was delighted, as, at nine years old, it allowed me to move closer to my childhood sweetheart and go to her house, *Wonder Years*–style, to play with her model farm animals; enact homespun dramas in a makeshift theatre in her front room; and be served tea and biscuits on a trolley by her mum, an infant school headmistress with her hair in a bun. We would have different kinds of neighbours now, including schoolteachers, salespersons, shopkeepers, and people in office jobs. Things were looking up. There was even talk of buying a second-hand car for runs out to the seaside. In Prime Minister Harold Macmillan's words, we had never had it so good.

Nature and Creativity

A year or so after we moved house, I went up to the top juniors and into Miss Hindle's class. The 1960s were not yet swinging, but child-centred education was emerging, and even by these standards, Mary Hindle was years ahead of her time.

My best teacher ever was, by then, past halfway in the forty-year career she'd spend entirely within the school. In a throwback world of inkwells and shoe inspections, she rarely used a blackboard, regularly involved students in small-group activities, and initiated the then unheard-of practice of allowing students to stay in class at playtime, or recess, and work on their projects if they wished, as many chose to do. Basics were covered, standards were high, and multiplication tables were recited on an almost daily basis, but literacy in particular was connected to students' interests, their passion for their group projects, and their engagements with the natural environment.

The 1959 report on Spring Hill from Her Majesty's Inspectors (HMI) praised how "written work is commendably neat and accurate; much of it is related to history, geography and nature study and is linked closely with the children's environment and interests." The nature table received special commendation. On the occasion of the school's centenary, Mary Hindle herself had fond recollections of "the nature groups: life, flowers, trees, birds, animals, insects etc." "Each group," she recalled, "worked and planned the work under a leader."[81]

Compare this to the early 2000s, when England was in the long unrelenting grip of standardized tests; intense concentration on literacy and numeracy; and the use of inspection reports to rank schools publicly and, if necessary, to justify external intervention. Gone were the references to the nature table. Instead, the inspectors wrote:

> *The teaching in literacy and numeracy lessons is effective and well-paced and meets the needs of children across the full ability range. A productive use of time and a brisk pace in the learning are significant features of the effective teaching.*[82]

Comments on science recorded how:

> *Pupils are provided with good opportunities to carry out practical investigations and solve problems. The majority of pupils are achieving the expected National Curriculum level by the end of Key Stage 1 although few are working at the higher level.*[83]

Attention to monitoring students' progress was clearly better in this kind of reporting, but somehow the magic and wonder of students' learning, and the inspired teaching that led to it, had disappeared.

Miss Hindle's classes offered more than just nature study, though. There were also the newspapers—four to a class. "The children worked in groups—each with its own editor [and] completely free to develop as the group wanted," she explained during the centenary celebration.[84] Anticipating my hyperactively itinerant future, perhaps, I took responsibility for the travel section of the *Friday Special*, writing about putatively exotic southern-English seaside resorts I had never visited that then defined the limits of my imagination.

There was also expressive free dance—or music and movement, as it was called. This working-class educational tradition for boys and girls alike began not with Billy Elliot but with famed social reformer Robert Owen in the 19th century school of New Lanark in Scotland.[85] Owen made dance a significant part of the curriculum for the children of his factory workers, along with the world's first provision of free early-childhood education. At Spring Hill, Mary Hindle recalled "the looks on many of the children's faces. . . . Some were completely absorbed in the music and the movement."[86]

Sometime in the 1990s, when Mary Hindle was in her ninth decade, I wrote to her in longhand, enclosing one of my published books. I explained that the short book in big print on the importance of teachers and teaching had been a bestseller over the years, reaching into six figures, with many foreign translations. Although she might not remember me, I wrote, I wanted her to know that she, more than anyone, had been a huge influence on my own decision to become an educator and on my own vision of what inspired teaching looked like. To the extent she had influenced me, I went on, she had also therefore influenced and inspired thousands of educators all over the world.

Replying in her own perfectly formed cursive script, Miss Hindle expressed her gratitude for the feedback. Right at the start of her letter, she said she did indeed remember me. Feeling like a child again, I turned over the page, wondering expectantly what might have stuck in her mind. Her sharpest recollection, it turned out, was not of my eleven-plus test scores or of other conventional academic achievements. "Am I right in thinking it was you who did a special Spanish dance?" she recalled—bringing back to life my proud and rebellious gypsy flamenco, pounded out in loud and rapid steps to the dramatic guitar rhythms and castanets of Cuban composer Ernesto Lecuona's "Malagueña"![87]

Discovery With Discipline

Mary Hindle was a quiet pioneer of the internationally famed British movement of progressive, or open, primary education that flourished in the 1960s and 1970s and that attracted educational visitors from the United States and all across the world.[88] Creative writing, groupwork, pupils' direction of their learning, and celebration of the arts and nature—these were the fruits of an age of optimism about children, as well as the future in education and society, of which I was an undoubted beneficiary. It was an educational age defined by a landmark report known as the Plowden Report and titled *Children and Their Primary Schools*.[89]

In the 21st century, policymakers and thought leaders are forever pointing to the educational challenges posed by a rapidly changing economy, by preparing children to change careers many times in their lifetimes for jobs that may not even exist yet. They highlight a world of increasing cultural diversity with the need to develop dispositions of empathy and tolerance and capacities to work with others. Gurus and global policy organizations point to new global competencies and 21st century skills as the mantra for what should define learning outcomes. This is what the Plowden Report already established in the 1960s, stating:

> *One obvious purpose is to fit children for the society into which they will grow up. To do this successfully it is necessary to predict what that society will be like. It will*

> *certainly be one marked by rapid and far reaching economic and social change. . . . More people will be called upon to change their occupation. About such a society we can be both hopeful and fearful. We can hope it will care for all its members . . . and that it will create an environment which is stimulating, honest and tolerant. We can fear that it will be much engrossed with the pursuit of material wealth, too hostile to minorities, too dominated by mass opinion and too uncertain of its values. For such a society, children, and the adults they will become, will need above all to be adaptable and capable of adjusting to their changing environment. They will need as always to be able to live with their fellows, appreciating and respecting their differences, understanding and sympathising with their feelings.*[90]

Unlike more modern reports about the purpose of education, though, the Plowden Report also talks about valuing children for what and who they are already are. Children are not merely adults-in-waiting, unformed hopes, or futures that are yet to come. They are, for almost twenty years—about a quarter of their lives—people with their own existence, needs, and contributions in their own right. Children have value not just because of what they will turn into but also because of the human nature of who they already are. Unlike many educational policy visions today that promote creativity and compassion, as well as literacy and numeracy, because of what people will need to be tomorrow, the Plowden Report also points to the needs of children as human beings in the present—just as Miss Hindle once did and as the best teachers still do:

> *A school . . . is a community in which children learn to live first and foremost as children and not as future adults. . . . The school sets out deliberately to devise the right environment for children, to allow them to be themselves and to develop in the way and at the pace appropriate to them. . . . It lays special stress on individual discovery, on first hand experience and on opportunities for creative work. It insists that knowledge does not fall into neatly*

> *separate compartments and that work and play are not opposite but complementary. A child brought up in such an atmosphere . . . has some hope of becoming a balanced and mature adult and of being able to live in, to contribute to, and to look critically at the society of which he forms a part. . . . The best preparation for being a happy and useful man or woman is to live fully as a child.*[91]

These ideas of valuing children as children are evident in the modern pushback against the excesses of standardized testing; in the movement by Martin Seligman and other experts in positive psychology to promote human flourishing, happiness, and well-being; and in the growing support for educating the whole child and the whole person, not just those bits of the person that can be employed, change jobs, and pass examinations.[92] As famous Buddhist guru Thích Nhât Hạnh advises, "Why wait to be happy?"[93]

Of course, letting children be children, advocating for more arts and creativity, and emphasizing a focus on the whole child in learning can evoke parental and public anxieties that rigour will be sacrificed for romanticism. Promoting human flourishing and well-being separately from academic achievement can echo the excesses of earlier reform movements, such as self-esteem, that showed no impact, or that even had a negative impact, on students' learning and development.[94] A backlash in favour of standards, accountability, direct instruction, and back to basics once more is as likely now as it would turn out to be from the late 1970s through the 1980s and beyond, after the global economy went into recession and child-centredness was attacked as economically unproductive and educationally ineffective self-indulgence.[95]

But the Plowden Report, like most other historic advocacies for progressive or democratic education such as that of U.S. educational philosopher John Dewey, does not present play as an alternative to hard work or discovery as the opposite of discipline. Dewey understood that education needed work *and* play, not one or the other.

Indeed, children's play is often hard work, and a lot of fulfilling work should feel like play.[96] The Plowden Report clearly states that it is wrong to claim that:

> *The older virtues, as they are usually called, of neatness, accuracy, care and perseverance, and the sheer knowledge which is an essential of being educated, will decline. . . . We repudiate the fear that the modern primary approach leads to their neglect. . . . Children need to be themselves, to live with other children and with grown ups, to learn from their environment, to enjoy the present, to get ready for the future, to create and to love, to learn to face adversity, to behave responsibly: in a word, to be human beings.*[97]

My classes in Spring Hill had music, drama, dance, and work on writing and on mathematics problems in small groups. But we also practised our multiplication tables, and from time to time, we would be called into the headmaster's office to demonstrate our capacities in mental arithmetic (rebranded today as mental agility). We lived and learned in that John Dewey–like world of *both–and*, not of ideologically divisive *either–or*.

Embracing the whole of me got the best out of me. If schools offer less than this, those who are privileged, advantaged, and tenacious can still find the grit to persevere and succeed. But children who neither come to school with these dispositions nor benefit from opportunities to experience whole-child education and support will flounder rather than flourish.

Expression and Distraction

Miss Hindle had a gift for accepting us for who we were, even when that included being naughty or mischievous. But she also prevented us from being *too much of it*. She knew how to balance the joys and excitement of discovery learning with the guidance and structures of discipline.

I couldn't have always been easy to teach. Although I was hard-working and enthusiastic, I was also the master of smart-aleck remarks and answering-back repartee. I was more than a bit head-strong sometimes, with an exaggerated sense of social injustice. I once lined up at her desk to complain about the way she had spoken to me in the schoolyard when she had misidentified me as the culprit of some infraction or another. She just quietly asked me to stand to one side while she figured out what to do (a one-week banishment to play outside with the younger children rather than work indoors on my projects).

My handwriting was, as it still is, indecipherable and messy, accompanied by inkblots all over the page. I was often late, always forgetting things, too talkative for my own good sometimes, and very fidgety. My mum and my grandparents used to call me things like "Daydreamer—off in his own world!" They complained that I had "Saint Vitus's dance" or, more prophetically, tagged me as the "absentminded professor." My exasperated mum would say things like "That lad will be late for his own funeral" and "He'd forget his 'ead if it were loose." More kindly, as was her nature, my grandma would react to the first signs of my hair loss in my twenties with the affirming "Grass doesn't grow on a busy street."

Miss Hindle hadn't failed to notice. Standing by her desk one day, I saw the report card she was writing on me and asked what "highly strung" meant! In those days, descriptions of this kind were not designed to inform any kind of remedial strategy but were simply set down as a pronouncement on a child's character that should be sorted out by the parents. Nowadays, being "highly strung" would be regarded as an identified disability of ADHD, which often leads to medication.

Miss Hindle, however, knew, professionally, how best to manage me without the kind of specific intervention that is now common. Because of this, I was able to grow and flourish and capitalize on the best, creative, and energetically driven parts of my highly strung personality without being suppressed by enforced calmness or pharmaceutical intervention. Indeed, in my letter back to Miss Hindle, more than three decades later, in my only "I told you so" moment, I wryly remarked that although I had often been in trouble in school for bad writing and too much talking, writing and talking had turned out to be the way I make my living.

In 2004, Miss Hindle was well into her eighties, and along with her lifelong partner, Miss Sutcliffe, the teacher in the class next door with whom she shared a home on the other side of town, she still went hill walking at the weekends. That year, I was approached to participate in one of the most moving events of my professional life. The old Victorian structure at Spring Hill was being demolished, and the governors of the school asked me whether I would come back and lay the foundation stone for the new building. I could not have imagined doing this without my best teacher. During the ceremony, Mary Hindle turned to my wife at one point and said, with a mixture of affection and exasperation, "How do you control him?" My wife lied. "I don't," she said. Which meant of course that this was exactly the way that she did!

In his bestselling book *The Element*, TED Talk legend Sir Ken Robinson shows how many successful artists often failed or got into trouble in school because of the very gifts that defined them as artists but made them hard to control in class—the drumming fingers of Mick Fleetwood of Fleetwood Mac or the constant spinning of Gillian Lynne, the choreographer for the musical *Cats*, for example.[98] Sir Ken is a brilliant intellectual, as well as a good friend, and he has got much more than half the argument about creativity completely right. In later years, though, when I came to do research on special education policy, I also gained overdue insight into why, throughout my adolescence and adult life, I had (like many other people), alongside my intellectual assets, suffered too much from debilitating bouts of anxiety, exhaustion, and depression that would have benefitted from some kind of earlier intervention to help me organize my things and manage my stress even just a bit.

As an adult, I have profited from my more restless, hyperactive qualities through great surges of creativity and a relentless work rate. I have felt able to see connections across ideas and disciplines that often evade others, to organize and improvise thoughts without notes in large public lectures, to talk myself out of trouble as quickly as I have talked myself into it, to deliver quick comebacks and make other people laugh, to inspire and enthuse others in pursuit of a common goal, and to undertake huge projects and initiatives that others often regard as impossible or unrealistic. Indeed, being told something won't work or can't be done is one of the greatest incentives I can be given to take it on. From time to time, in all kinds of ways, physically and professionally, I like to have a go at things that scare me a bit (in fact, I'm writing this after having returned to the exact spot where, a year ago, I broke my ankle and had a night-time mountain rescue on one of the most isolated sections of the U.S. Appalachian Trail).

But the debates over the existence or importance of ADHD are ones not only of underrecognizing children's creative capacities on the one hand or of overdiagnosing their disruptive gifts as psychological disorders on the other. There is a *both–and* element to this as there is to many other educational issues. Many years into my adulthood, when I was well into my fifties, my wife, a school administrator, was reading a book on adult ADHD by one of the biggest experts in the field, to try to help her support the students in her school who seemed to suffer from similar disorders.[99] "My God," she exclaimed, "this book's all about you!"

The unusual aspects of my character have certainly enabled me to succeed and be fulfilled in all kinds of ways. But they have also subjected me from an early age to darker periods of emotional turmoil.

It's good to have creative ideas. It's not good to be awake night after night with so many new ideas racing through your head that it physically hurts. Hard work is a virtue. But it is not healthy when you feel such intolerable strain—from the burden of undertaking what seems utterly overwhelming, or from confronting the prospect of letting everybody down—that you bang your head against the wall to inflict a more manageable physical pain instead. I understand all too easily the dangerous attractions that others sometimes find in self-harming. Quips and banter can be entertaining, but constantly interrupting rather than merely overlapping other people's sentences because you can't wait for the end of them can be hurtful and insulting. So too can having your mind wander off into a string of idiosyncratic associations when someone else—a colleague, a friend, or a family member—just wants you to listen properly. My expectations for myself could be and sometimes still are brutal, but so too, sometimes, have been the incredibly high expectations I set for others. And witnessing a neat pile of your papers turning into a mountain of chaos within minutes in a meeting, despite the use of ring binders, colour coding, or Perspex holders, can damage your contribution to the meeting and give others the impression you are incompetent, can't be bothered, or don't really care.

A few sessions of life-changing counselling after my wife's revelation helped me realize, as my counsellor told me, that mostly, I had, through life, devised ways to manage my weaknesses to capitalize on my strengths. For one thing, I had married a partner who loved me for what I am and who could also help organize me and protect me from my excesses. I had intuitively built teams that included others with capacities that I lacked—to arrange information, maintain effective written communication with others, establish timelines, interpret spreadsheets, make good-natured fun of my flaws, get me to be a bit more diplomatic and stop blurting things out, and so on. I paradoxically became a well-regarded and globally successful workshop presenter because I knew I had to build in carefully designed protocols ensuring that others would get their rightful opportunities to participate and to have a voice without my hogging the stage.

But, my counsellor pointed out, in the midst of a serious depression when I had thought that just a quick flick of my car steering wheel would stop my being a burden on everybody and constantly letting them down, I also needed to tell others about some of the things that defined me so that they wouldn't just see me as someone who was inconsiderate and inept. So I have colleagues now who will kindly help me locate the right papers in the midst of a key meeting—including ones I am chairing that involve ministers of state and other dignitaries. Before I walk into a reception or a social—a kind of event that scares me with the prospect of saying the wrong things to the wrong people whose illustrious names I have also forgotten—my wife, Pauline, or a colleague will brief me on who is in the room, what I should remember about them, and how I should address them. Every so often, my counsellor advised me, when I couldn't stop worrying and my anxieties overwhelmed me, I should also take an antianxiety medication just to reduce the intensity a bit—something I now do a few times a year (and that once got me through delivering a nerve-racking TEDx Talk to more than a thousand people in Brazil).[100] And also, he concluded, to avoid excess worry about not getting things perfect, as well as feelings of unwarranted regret—an emotion I can waste on the most trivial things, like having chosen the wrong item off the menu!—I should try to be less hard on myself sometimes.

In the years following these counselling sessions, in general, my professional and personal relationships have improved, and this has benefitted others, as well as myself. I have become a better and more willing leader because I no longer feel I am hiding who I truly am all the time and because others are now able to help me be the best I can be for them, while offsetting those aspects of myself that interfere with or interrupt this goal. I have learned to be true to myself but to avoid being too much of it, and to be open with others about my limitations, as well as my strengths, so we can all be better at what we have to do together. And unlike most of the top-down and usually male leaders who once were in charge of me, I am now having some success at passing on these ways of leading to the generation of leaders after me.

Miss Hindle was really the first of my teachers to understand how to balance discovery with discipline and how to enable students like me to be ourselves without going over the top. The existential irony of all this can be captured in the story of the school bell.

The Bell That Tolled for Me

By the time we reached the top juniors, many of us were given formal jobs or responsibilities. We were called monitors, after the 19th century monitorial system in England where older students would perform subsidiary and supervisory tasks for their teachers. The plant monitor watered the plants. The window monitor would wield an improbably long and heavy pole to open and close the windows high above us all. I had one of the best jobs. I was the bell monitor. At the appropriate and exact time, I had to ring the old-fashioned brass school bell at the start and end of the school day, at playtimes, and at lunchtimes so students knew when to come in and when to leave. What could be simpler and more impressive than that? What could possibly go wrong?

The school hadn't considered my distinctive sense of my own responsibilities. One day, I looked up at the clock—none of us had watches or phones then—and rang the bell for playtime. Throughout the school, students got up from their desks and started to file out into the hallway and the yard. Teachers, with upcoming time commitments I knew nothing about and a schedule to accommodate them—a staff meeting or a visit from the school nurse, perhaps—made futile efforts to stop them. For a few minutes, chaos and havoc reigned.

Once this was all over, Miss Hindle took me to one side and explained that I had to ask the teacher's permission to ring the bell, as it was the teacher who knew when it was the right time. In my own mind, though, I knew when playtime was and when the bell should be rung for it. I was the bell monitor, not them. My responsibility was to ring the bell, and I rang it. Why have a dog and bark yourself?

My own reasoning was of no use. Miss Hindle asked me to apologize. I wouldn't. They sent me to the headmaster to make me apologize. I refused. They brought in my parents and sat with me and with them to make me see sense. I still wouldn't apologize. I can't remember what exactly happened next, but my resuming bell-ringing duties was definitely not part of it. I would never be allowed to ring the school bell again—at least, not for a very long time.

In 2004, at the end of the foundation-stone-laying ceremony at Spring Hill, with Miss Hindle, the local newspaper, and my mother (very impressed by the fact that I'd made the local paper and was now, finally, indisputably famous!) all present, I was given a thank-you gift. It was the original old school bell, complete with a crack down one side and a repaired clapper. "Clapper Happy," the *Lancashire Evening Telegraph* proclaimed, with a picture of me ringing the bell once more.[101] But best of all, in a box under the bell was a brief and telling message that now, after all these years, I could ring the bell anywhere, anytime, for any reason, in a manner of my own choosing.

Primary Lessons

Some of the best lessons are the ones we learn in our earliest years in school, even if they do not sink in for a long time. Let students be themselves or become the better part of themselves, but don't let them get away with anything they want. Beware of channelling students into life-shaping paths too early. Understand that creativity and self-expression will sometimes be a bit disruptive for the conventional class environment. Balance and integrate discovery with direction, work with play, exploration with repetition. In all of this, show consideration and kindness to every student, even when you don't approve of what he or she might have done. Do this for all students but especially for those who struggle the most with their learning or their lives.

Inspire the young minds that are given to you, for you never know whom they might be able to inspire in turn in the future. In the words of the late Canadian poet and singer Leonard Cohen:

> *Ring the bells that still can ring.*
> *Forget your perfect offering.*
> *There is a crack, a crack, in everything.*
> *That's how the light gets in.*[102]

CHAPTER 4

End of Eden

It is the class system that really lies at the root of our problems.

—Tony Benn

In 1963, when I was twelve years old, there was a sudden change in our family's fortunes. My dad died from his third heart attack. It was May—the same month my mum was born. She was just forty-three years old. The only good thing was that my dad's heart attack happened a few months after—and not just before—the selective test that would determine whether I would go to grammar school. Had he died immediately before the test, I might never have passed it.

Tests that have high stakes for accountability are one of the biggest educational issues of our time. But before that, and still, in many countries today, tests and examinations have had another kind of high stakes—for selection for schools and pathways that will, in many respects, decide young people's entire futures. Tests and exams now usually have this purpose and effect near or at the end of high school, to decide eligibility for university. In my childhood, these tests took place as early as age eleven—and, if we include tests used for allocation to higher and lower streams or tracks, even earlier.

The Time of Tests

A year or so before we lost my dad, the prospect and pressure of the upcoming eleven-plus test had clearly been taking its toll on me, though I denied it at the time. My brothers couldn't get me to play outside. I'd lost all my energy. I would sit for ages, hunched over the coal fire, staring into the flames. I was pale as a ghost. Our family doctor took blood tests for anaemia and leukaemia. My parents purchased jars of a substance called Virol (it looked like Marmite and was also a by-product of the brewing industry) so I could ingest daily spoonfuls of malt-flavoured vitamins. Like other children who seemed not to be thriving, I was prescribed a sunlamp—the fad cure at the time, though one that would bring many users skin cancer in their middle age—so that for a few hours a week I could be exposed to recuperative beams of heat and light. My mum and dad even sent me away for a week to a country manor used by the local council to provide holidays for children whose hard-up families couldn't afford them. Showing little gratitude, and exhibiting my customary inclinations to protest against unfairness or unnecessary restriction, I experienced this as being more like a prison camp and rebelled against it to the point where my parents had to come and take me home.

Students' anxiety about examinations and tests has become one of the reasons for opposition to them and for their overthrow in the 21st century. In South Korea, for example, the high-stakes assessments on which entrance to a top-three university depends are widely regarded as condemning students to "Examination Hell."[103] As well as South Korea, other East Asian systems such as Hong Kong and China have been experiencing increasing rates of adolescent suicides in the face of examination pressures.[104] A "shadow" system of private after-school tutoring that sits alongside the regular schooling system—enabling advantaged families to get their children to the best university possible—consumes endless hours of students' time with test preparation that has no relation to creativity, modern work skills, problem-solving skills, or preparation to live in a civil society.[105] The 2017 results of an OECD study on student well-being found that the countries that placed the highest emphasis on standardized testing also recorded the lowest levels of self-reported student happiness.[106] In England, Diane Reay is one of many researchers who have documented how these negative side effects of testing are not distributed evenly across all students but harm those from working-class backgrounds more than from any other group.[107] Another Diane—Ravitch—has campaigned relentlessly with others against these negative effects of testing in the United States.[108]

Even in Ontario, Canada, which has less testing than England and most U.S. states, a 2017 evaluation I conducted with my colleagues of one-seventh of the school districts and their responses to educational reform revealed serious concerns about the impact of high-stakes testing in grades 3 and 6 on innovation, equity in students' learning, and students' well-being.[109] An indigenous community leader I worked with on a government committee—that, following the emerging evidence of our research, was subsequently established to review the province's assessment system—told the rest of us that when the tests were handed out, teachers on her First Nations reserve wore rubber gloves because some students' anxiety about the test was so great they vomited all over their papers.

There is no need to keep subjecting young students to the kind of test anxieties that were inflicted on me and many of my young peers in the 1960s and that affect disadvantaged students disproportionately more than a half century later. Why try to inspire and educate students with 21st century teaching and learning when we are still subjecting them to a 20th century system of assessment? It's time for assessment policies and practices in our schools to catch up and move on.

Three Types of Minds

The eleven-plus exam was designed to select students at the end of primary school for one of three kinds of secondary schools—grammar schools for the top 10–20 per cent, depending on the area where they lived; technical schools for a tiny percentage of students in the middle; and secondary modern schools for the vast remainder.

Just before the United Kingdom's 1944 Education Act, which would provide universal secondary education up to age fifteen, a government report known as the Norwood Report laid the foundation for three "broad types of education" in secondary schools. These were meant to correspond to three types of students whose occupational futures could be anticipated and predicted by the selection test.[110] Without any recourse to expertise or evidence, the report's committee and its chair, Sir Cyril Norwood—former headmaster of Harrow, one of the country's top two independent, or private, schools—arrogantly asserted that these "rough groupings . . . have in fact established themselves in general educational experience."[111] The report then went on to describe three types of students, or minds, and the type of secondary education that would be appropriate for each of them. First was:

> *The pupil who is interested in learning for its own sake, who can grasp an argument or follow a piece of connected reasoning, who is interested in causes . . . who cares to know how things came to be as well as how they are, who is sensitive to language as expression of thought, to a proof as a precise demonstration, to a series of experiments justifying a principle: he is interested in the relatedness of related things, in development, in structure, in a coherent body of knowledge. . . . Such pupils, educated by the curriculum commonly associated with the Grammar School, have entered the learned professions or have taken up higher administrative or business posts.*[112]

Second was:

> *The pupil whose interests and abilities lie markedly in the field of applied science or applied art. The boy in this group has . . . the necessary qualities of mind to carry his interest through to make it his life work at whatever level of achievement. He often has an uncanny insight into the intricacies of mechanism whereas the subtleties of language construction are too delicate for him. To justify itself to his mind, knowledge must be capable of immediate application. . . . The various kinds of technical school were . . . instituted to prepare boys and girls for taking up certain crafts—engineering, agriculture and the like.*[113]

In the third and most numerous group was:

> *The pupil [who] deals more easily with concrete things than with ideas. He may have much ability, but it will be in the realm of facts. He is interested in things as they are; he finds little attraction in the past or in the slow disentanglement of causes or movements. His mind must turn its knowledge or its curiosity to immediate test; and his test is essentially practical. . . . Because he is interested only in the moment he may be incapable of a long series of connected steps; relevance to present concerns is the only way of awakening interest, abstractions mean little to him.*[114]

Each type of mind would be provided with an associated type of curriculum. The grammar schools would have an abstract curriculum that "treats the various fields of knowledge as suitable for coherent and systematic study *for their own sake*."[115] In the proposed technical schools, of which only a tiny number were eventually created, the curriculum would concentrate on "the special data and skills associated with a particular kind of occupation . . . related to industry, trades and commerce."[116] The third type of curriculum would provide not education, as such, but training that would "enable pupils to take up the work of life" by "practical touch with affairs."[117] Three types of minds for three kinds of schools and three social classes—this was the new way to perpetuate the British class system in a nutshell. Not only was it a report about fitting young people into the bowler hat, trilby, and flatcap of upper-, middle-, and working-class male society. It was one in which girls didn't appear at all.

In places like Ontario, Canada, where I am living once more, these kinds of class-related distinctions still persist in the form of academic and applied tracks, or streams, along with "place-based" learning, focused on the local community, for the lowest track of all. And in England, before its political life became consumed with Brexit, Prime Minister Theresa May made fitful efforts to expand the number of grammar schools or student places within those schools.[118] In doing so, she failed to bring to the public's attention that there is no overall evidence that a grammar school system provides superior levels of achievement or equity to a fully comprehensive system—and that more grammar schools for a few means more de facto secondary modern schools for all the rest.

In England, in 2013, research conducted for the Sutton Trust found that "in local authorities that operate the grammar system, children who are not eligible for free school meals have a much greater chance of attending a grammar school than similarly high achieving children who are eligible for free school meals."[119] In addition, the heads of grammar schools have said that "parents from disadvantaged backgrounds often associate their schools with tradition, middle class values and elitism" and are less inclined to send their children there as a result.[120]

My brothers and I were the living embodiments of the tripartite grammar school system. Peter, Colin, and I were born three years apart from each other. Peter, the eldest, went to secondary modern school, destined to leave at age fifteen with no qualifications—as the secondary moderns didn't offer any at the time—to become an apprentice toolmaker in a local factory. The reason he failed his exam was that he walked out in protest in the middle of it when his effort to borrow a rubber, or eraser, from another student was interpreted as cheating (he did not disclose this to our mum until she was in her eighties!). Pete eventually overcame this setback through his own self-made-man narrative involving night-school classes in drafting, followed by emigration to Canada, where he eventually established his own business of installing environmental-pollution-control systems. But the stigma of having been channelled into an unsuitable and unfulfilling education at just eleven years old still stuck in his gullet.

When Pete and I were both in our fifties, and attempting to fix something together, I said, "I envy you. You have such a gift for this kind of thing. It comes naturally to you."

There I was with my own "three types of minds" talk!

"I have no gift for it at all," he fired back. "My gifts are in painting, singing opera, and history. All the manual skills I have, I had to learn them the hard way because I had no other choice."

Pete was always very musical. As an infant, he would stand on a chair and conduct imaginary orchestras in the backyard. He took up violin lessons with the best music teacher in town, but he never picked up a violin again after he carried his instrument in its case to his secondary modern school and got a beating for it. When he left school, he turned to the harmonica and also adopted the long working-class tradition of playing the spoons and the bones (discarded by the local butcher)—the castanets of the northern-English working man—on his hands and thighs. Pete also loved to listen to classical and popular tenors like Beniamino Gigli, Mario Lanza, and, later, Luciano Pavarotti. In middle age, he practised for and performed in a number of amateur operas. But at eleven, because of a single and sullied test event, he was condemned to work with his hands even though he was not really fitted for that kind of work at all.

Colin was the middle child, and he took the middle path—a technical school for youngsters who would be headed into trades, technical drawing, and routine clerical work. Colin also had some musical talents in violin and harmonica, but his real passion was for sport. The Norwood Report had no type of child for that—or for many other things, in fact. All three of us were reasonably adept at football and cricket. But Colin had a special ability at cricket as a bowler. He could make a ball swing one way in the air, like a curveball in baseball, and then get it to cut back off the pitch in the opposite direction. And he was fast. If I or anyone else took liberties with his bowling and hit him for a few runs, we would find the next ball whistling around our ears or pounding into our ribs. Pete still talks about the fractures to his fingers and ribs that were the physical evidence of all this.

Colin was in the same class at school as future England cricket captain and TV commentator David Lloyd and reckoned he could bowl him out and match him for skill. But when they went on to play in local club cricket, Colin recalled, while Lloyd and others from more advantaged homes on the other side of town could afford the equipment and make it to the matches and the practices, Colin found that his limited financial resources and subsequent factory-work commitments made it hard for him to benefit from what his club could offer. So he dropped his sport, went to work in another local factory, and married early, when he was still in his teens.

In later years, I learned that my dad had always wanted one of us to go to university and get the chance he never had. I was now the family's last hope. I don't recall there ever being any overt pressure for me to pass the eleven-plus—only my mum reassuring me often, as many working-class parents did, that it wouldn't be "the end of the world" if I didn't get through. Of course, the prevalence of this narrative amongst parents and their children, and the need they felt to say it, was itself strangely indicative of the brutal truth of the very opposite. On the day the results came out, I stood expectantly on the street corner, waiting to ambush the postman. He handed me a long brown envelope that contained the news that would shape my life forever. I tore it open, looked at the contents, and ran inside the house to tell my mum. "I've passed! I've passed!" I shouted. And off to grammar school I went.

X, L, and S

I enjoyed most of my first year in grammar school. I still had some friends from my old school, and now I had new ones as well. Our teachers, in their academic gowns that aped the independent-school tradition, were not especially inspiring, though. Dozy Ken, the religious studies teacher, was named after his unusual capacity to fall asleep midsentence. Our history teacher gained perverse pleasure in punishing boys for not wearing their caps at all times to and from school. He once gave a zero to another boy for copying a camel he had drawn on the blackboard facing left to right instead of right to left as he had drawn it. Another hapless teacher was a prime target for inverse bullying that took the form of a merciless string of practical jokes.

British boys' secondary schools in the 1960s had been largely staffed by an army of men looking for work upon returning from World War II. As Margaret Drabble describes poignantly in her semiautobiographical novel *The Radiant Way*, these men, with just a shot of emergency training, took away secondary school teaching jobs from capable and qualified women who had comprised much of the teaching profession during wartime.[121]

Our better teachers were, indeed, mainly women. And my geography teacher, Ma Waring, was ahead of them all. She inspired me to take up geography and was the first teacher to help me realize I had creative capacities when she fed back to me that I had come up with a completely new classification for lakes (though what she didn't add was whether it was a good one!). She would sit on one of the desks at the front and, in a truly touching way, reflect on the meaning of her own life, including how people like herself coped after the loss of a loved one.

On one unforgettable occasion, when I had decided to stay home for a few days' unauthorized absence to revise for my A-level, or university-entrance, examinations, I went out at lunchtime to investigate the sound of banging on the back door at the end of our yard. I thought I needed to let in the coalman. When I unbolted the door, however, I came face-to-face with my geography teacher. She had been unable to make herself heard at the front because I was playing loud rock music on my tape recorder. Entering our tiny living room, she looked askance at my brother's new wife, fully made up and wearing a scarlet velvet dress. My sister-in-law tried waving her wedding-ring finger in the air to counter the impression that she might have been my girlfriend! After all this, Mrs. Waring didn't rant and rave, criticize or cajole, but calmly suggested it might be a good idea for me to return to school now and complete my studying there—which I duly did, going on to win the school geography prize several months later.

By contrast, many of the male teachers, bearing the psychological, as well as physical, scars of battle, had little talent for teaching and even less interest in or empathy for adolescents. Boys' secondary schools like mine were consequently characterized by strictness, sarcasm, canings, and cruelty. The boys didn't need to do the bullying; the teachers did it for them! Our science teacher was not alone in choosing to read the percentage scores for our work out loud, beginning with the boys with the lowest numbers, so that those near the end of the list would be grateful just to scrape 50 per cent, which turned out to be almost the top score. One of our French teachers would wade through the desks showering hails of spit through his nicotine-stained teeth to drag out boys who had been talking from the back row. The other teacher of French nicknamed me "Toothy" after my two broken front teeth, and he made me and other boys sit under his desk if we were caught talking out of turn. No wonder I developed a lifelong aversion to learning "foreign" languages.

Worse than all this, though, was the sheer drudgery of classroom learning. After the self-direction and collaborative groupwork of primary school came dreary repetitions of lecturing, dictation of notes, and regimented whole-class teaching. Mathematics classes were so tedious we entertained ourselves by counting how many times the teacher would say "yes, yes" to punctuate his sentences (the winning total was in excess of forty—more than one a minute). With the weakest and least-vigilant teachers, these lessons could at least be mitigated by games of cards, shove-halfpenny on our desktops, or superhero comics read surreptitiously at the back of the class. But mostly, achievement had to overcome the absence of any engagement. This was dogged endurance, or *grit*, long before Angela Duckworth called it that.[122]

Despite all this, I still did well and, except for science, was near the top of the class in almost everything, including ranking first in Latin and mathematics. At the end of year 1, we were separated into three further groups, or streams. Those assigned to the X class—the Express stream—did the four-year course for the General Certificate of Education (GCE) in three years. Those in the L class had to take the usual four years but were allowed to continue with the privilege of studying Latin. Those in the S stream were deemed too stupid to continue with Latin and were assigned to do extra science instead—largely physics and chemistry, as biology was still regarded as a girls' subject then. In a nation where C. P. Snow's "two cultures" of arts and science were alive and well,[123] and in a time before STEM (science, technology, engineering, and mathematics) became fashionable, British students who went on to university to study sciences, especially applied sciences like engineering, were snootily regarded by their peers, including me, as academically and socially inferior to everyone else.

In the next two years or so, though, my results were less impressive. Decades later, when I pored over these old report cards with my wife in our basement in Canada and wondered aloud what went wrong in those years, her answer was "It's obvious. Your dad died." For me, after the inspiration of Mary Hindle, then the excitement of being in a new school and top of the form in a number of things, the end of the first year in grammar school was like the end of Eden.

Home Truths

My memory of my relationship with my dad is not as vivid as my brothers' memories of him. Being a bit older, my brothers had got the best years out of him. For example, Dad taught Colin to use both feet as a football player by making him wear a soft plimsoll rather than a boot on his stronger right foot so that he would learn to kick the rock-hard, laced-up ball with his weaker left foot instead. This developed his strength in both feet so he would become a rare two-footed player.

With me being the youngest son, by the time I was ready to play like this, my dad had already had two heart attacks, beginning at age forty-three. In those days, the medical wisdom was that heart-attack victims should be metaphorically wrapped in cotton wool and exercise as little as possible. So my memories of my dad are not of football practice but of paperwork and invoices, which I helped him organize and process when he brought his work as a warehouse manager home with him in the evenings. The only physical engagement I recall was when we were play-fighting on the floor and he collapsed in agony. I felt sure I had killed him, but all I had actually done was kick him in the testicles!

My dad's last heart attack began inconspicuously but not uncommonly when he strained himself on the outdoor toilet. He immediately took to his bed, which by then was downstairs in our living room, until the ambulance came and drove him and my mother to Blackburn Royal Infirmary. I remember looking through the bedroom window and watching it leave after they had loaded him in, wondering whether that would be the last I would ever see of him. It was. Colin and I shared my mum's double bed that night, huddled under the candlewick bedspread. In the middle of us messing about the next morning, my mum came back with the bad news.

We cried, all of us—except for Peter, the eldest, who stoically refused. There was a funeral a few days later, but in order to try to protect me, the sensitive youngest one, they didn't allow me to attend, say goodbye, or physically confront the fact that he was gone. For at least two or three years, when I had some good news, like exam results, my first thought was always "I must tell Dad." For a longer time after that, well into my thirties, I had the most vivid uplifting dreams, almost like visions, that he had come back alive, to be with us. I would wake up in ecstasy only for the cruel truth to sink in again.

Dad's death was a blow to me, for sure. For Mum, it was utterly devastating. Her children were growing up, and she and my dad had been looking forward to having some time together—nothing fancy, just a night or two out to the pub, trips to the seaside, and a little car for holidays. But all that was gone now. So too was money and security. Mum took most of my dad's small pension as a lump sum to pay off the mortgage—to keep a roof over our heads, as she put it, bricks and mortar. She went back to work and struggled on with her collection of part-time jobs, making the best of it, as working-class widows did. For a while, all this got her through.

At first, Peter and Colin were working and bringing their pay packets home. We formed an odd bond as brothers. Football up the park with other lads from the neighbourhood—whatever the weather, including the annual ritual of playing on frozen pitches on Boxing Day—saw us coming back home gleefully covered in mud to our mum's disgusted calls of "Get them filthy things off, and put 'em in t' wash."

Every other winter Saturday, we also went to watch Burnley, then one of the top teams in England, at the local football game. With our mum out working at the co-op, my brothers and I had our Saturday-morning ritual: commando fights with clothes-pegs on the living-room carpet; hot meat-and-potato pies from the corner shop at the bottom of our street; the walk downhill to catch the bus and ride on the top deck, six miles to the match; then the last half-mile walk through the gathering crowds to the turnstiles and on into the ground.

Flatcaps and overcoats; being packed like sardines between ranks of men seemingly twice my height; peering through the gaps for a glimpse of the actual play; stamping frozen feet in thin-soled shoes to mitigate the numbness from the icy cold; a flask of coffee at half-time, with an illicit shot of rum to warm the cockles; the crushing press of swaying bodies when a corner kick was being taken or a shot was made at goal. All these things stay strong in my memory still and have left me with an utterly irrational lifelong loyalty—win, lose, or draw—to Burnley Football Club, my local team.[124]

In his own ham-fisted way, Peter, my eldest brother, also stepped up to take the place of my dad in some respects. He introduced me to walking through the hills, over the moors, mile after mile, rain or shine. It's a passion that has stayed with both of us ever since. Off he would take me for up to twenty miles, through heath and bog, with only school shoes on my feet. But this got us both outdoors, kept us occupied, and laid the foundation for an obsession I still have for hiking long-distance trails across the continents of the world. These years of getting by after my dad had gone didn't last, though. A series of crises and losses would soon follow.

Peter had a terrifying seizure and spent three days in hospital unconscious after a serious concussion playing in goal at football. Then he broke the same leg three times in succession—the last one during an ill-advised effort to crouch down to play lawn bowling

"She could still do cartwheels into her sixties." My mum as a young woman showing off her physical skills.

Doris and Albert (Mum and Dad), with me (left)—before onesies—and my brothers.

"School uniforms and caps were always spick and span," even on holiday. Peter and Colin are firing cannons at the back. I'm at the front, reflecting on the wisdom of it.

"My old primary school playmate—the front half of God" (bottom right), with me playing the back half behind her shoulder. Spring Hill school choir, 1959/60.

"I was a wiry kid," winning no Charles Atlas contests on the beach on summer holiday.

"I . . . never heard her say a harsh word about anyone." My grandma—as spellbound by a fairground organ as our one-year-old son, Stuart.

"Way back in the corner . . . sporting a big black eye, is me."
My brother Colin's wedding on FA Cup Final day, 1967.

Me and my "curly muttonchop sideburns—or Mungo Jerries" during Peter's first visit back home, with his Canadian fiancée, Shirley (left).

"I . . . wrote and sang some of the songs." The Nook Band, left to right: Bob, Macca, Barry, Ges—and me.

"'Don't be silly,' she responded." My future wife, Pauline, at the end of the boat landing where I proposed, with no ring, in 1972.

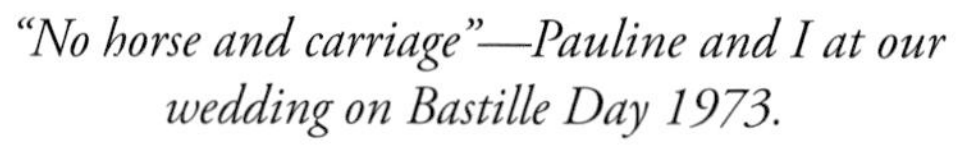

"No horse and carriage"—Pauline and I at our wedding on Bastille Day 1973.

"Peter, Colin, and I were born three years apart from each other," but later we all sported seedy moustaches, '70s-style.

"I could ring the bell anywhere, anytime"—best of all, with my former teacher Mary Hindle at Spring Hill's foundation-stone-laying ceremony in 2004.

while still wearing his plaster cast from his previous two fractures! Eventually, he recovered, but by the time he reached twenty-one and I was fourteen, he decided to spend his carefully earned savings on emigrating to Canada. We all went on the train with him to Liverpool, where he boarded a ship for its last transatlantic voyage. My mum was heartbroken. He was her eldest son, her firstborn, and none of us thought we would ever see him again.

Colin, meanwhile, was bringing his own kind of problems. He was hanging around with a rough element now, getting into trouble at work and in danger of getting on the wrong side of the law (though when he became a policeman a few years later, he realized this misspent youth had been good training!). Then he met Elaine, a blonde-bombshell factory worker who was nonetheless steady, shy, and quiet and who started to settle him down. Everything seemed to be looking up until they came home one day and announced that Elaine was pregnant and they would have to get married. Shotgun marriages, as they were called in those days, brought disgrace on a respectable working family, and my mother was beside herself with disappointment and shame—even though Elaine tragically lost their child when it had been carried to full term.

Mum had lost her husband; been brought to the brink of poverty; and faced crisis, shame, and yet more losses in the case of two of her sons. Finally, when I was fifteen, she collapsed in what was then described as a nervous breakdown. She could carry on no longer. Peter was gone, Colin was out at work, and for months on end, more than a year perhaps, Mum practically stopped eating anything other than a powder formula called Complan. She took to her bed for days at a time and was then struck down with a series of illnesses—anaemia that required iron injections; an infected gallbladder that had to be removed; and chronic insomnia for which she was prescribed barbiturates, which she was only able to abandon after several years. She also developed agoraphobia that was so severe even the shortest bus ride would provoke uncontrollable shaking.

I don't remember a moment when I thought, "I'd better do something about this." In our class and culture, we worked things out for ourselves in a very practical way and simply tried to make the best of things. So after talking to my grandma, I began a new routine.

My grandma was the extended working-class family personified. She was always available for anyone who needed her—a bit of shopping if you didn't have time to do it yourself; a sympathetic ear and a cup of tea when you had a problem or were upset; an afternoon run out to the seaside with her husband in his old Austin 8 jalopy if you were feeling a bit down; and willingness to come round and help out, at the drop of a hat, if you were sick and couldn't get out of bed or leave the house. In my entire life, I only ever saw my grandma exude kindness and never heard her say a harsh word about anyone—except for the torrents of profanity she hurled at wrestlers like Mick McManus and Jackie Pallo, just before the reading of the football results, on Saturday-afternoon TV.

When my mum became seriously ill, my grandma would come up about eleven o'clock to take care of everything after she had put her own house in order. So every morning, I had to pitch in myself. After Colin had gone off to work, I'd get up, make breakfast, and then set and light the fire with firewood, coal, and newspapers. I used to enjoy this fire-making moment—putting the steel blower up in front of the fire, with sheets of newspaper spread out to cover the gaps at the side, then seeing the flames behind the paper roar up the chimney with the draught drawn underneath. Then came the dusting and vacuum-cleaning—or *hoovering up*, as we called it—front room and back. After this, every day, in a time before supermarkets, I would head out with a shopping list to pick up some "best end of neck" or "two lean loin pork chops" (I used to say this in a sniggering way) from the local butcher, who would share a few jokes of the trade with me, like "Have you got pigs' trotters?" "No, I always walk like this!"

On the way back, I'd collect fresh vegetables like a cabbage or some carrots and turnips and bring them home. I got quite adept at picking the prime cuts of meat and rejecting vegetables or fruit that were not at their best—skills that would serve me well when, a couple of years later, I worked on a market stall on Saturdays and two evenings a week to earn a bit of pocket money. When I'd done, my grandma would come up to cook lunch, or dinner, as we called it, and I would then head off to school, getting there between ten and eleven in the morning without a single comment or question from any of my teachers.

Slowly, my mum started to recover. I got her off the formula, made her get out of bed, and began to escort her out and back on trips at night to see her women friends. As a teenage boy, though, I instinctively knew enough about Sigmund Freud's Oedipus complex to draw the line at walking alongside her, insisting instead on accompanying her unobtrusively, in the shadows, on the opposite side of the street.

With my mum still no longer working, and her sick pay running out, we were forced onto welfare benefits. My black corduroy jacket for going out in had to double as my school uniform—something my teachers didn't always appreciate. My overcoat was a hand-me-down from my mum's friend's son. I also remember going with Mum downtown to the social-security office by the bus station and witnessing the shame she felt in having to rely on what she regarded as charity. "I never thought it would come to this," she used to say despairingly. We were a lone-parent family now, with very little income. We weren't starving, but we were definitely struggling.

Missed Opportunities

My school never punished me for my lateness that was recorded at the start of each school day and that therefore turned into official prolonged absences—so they must have known what was going on.

But they never talked to me directly about my dad's death, how my mum was doing, or how I was coping either. All I recall was an unexpected visit from the truancy officer. My school reports, however, showed telltale signs that I was starting to fall behind. In English, I had to "guard against carelessness." Physics and geography were "disappointing" and "very disappointing," respectively. By the time I was fifteen, absences had become a problem—twenty-five, or five weeks' worth, in one term—and were seriously affecting my performance. My Latin teacher, for example, complained that I was "capable of a better result." To my face, the French teacher was less diplomatic. "Not only will you fail French," he proclaimed. "You will fail miserably."

Given the conventional school timetable, where hard subjects come in the morning and easier ones in the afternoon, one subject I missed a lot because of my late starts was mathematics. My arithmetic and basic computation had always been excellent, and from the age of eight or nine, I had been able to impress local shopkeepers with my ability to add up long lists of shopping items in my head before they had done it by hand or on their adding machines. But now, mathematics meant algebra, calculus, and trigonometry. They went in sequence. Miss one lesson, and you couldn't follow the next. It was the same with Latin. Soon, in any test or an exam, I was not only unable to answer the questions. I didn't even understand what the questions meant.

Until I entered my sixties, one of my most frequent anxiety dreams involved mathematics classes: I would arrive at school for a test, often late, turn over the page, and be unable to recognize a single question. Variations of this dream had me wandering about the vaguely familiar school, completely unable to find my class, where I knew an exam was about to start. In some of these I was a child again; in others an adult amongst children. In either case, I would wake up in hot sweats and take quite some time to grasp that what I had just dreamed was not real.

Finally, just a few years ago, I put these dreams to rest when I started including mathematics activities in my workshops with teachers. Without realizing it, in beginning to own my mathematics problems and potential, I was adopting Carol Dweck's growth mindset —that I was just not a mathematics person *yet.*[125] Now mathematics no longer stalks me, I have discovered to my surprise, and my anxiety dreams have developed new themes instead.

Class Matters

There are many reasons why children in working-class families don't do as well in school as their middle-class counterparts. Studies on both sides of the Atlantic have been documenting these inequities for fifty years.[126] The oldest explanation was that it was just genetic inheritance—the same one that wrongly explained the differences between black and white children. Others pointed to family upbringing and lack of parental interest or involvement, though my parents, like many of their working-class counterparts, took us regularly to the public library and encouraged us to complete our homework and even take on further activities. Then there are other things that come with modest financial circumstances that make it harder to cope in working-class families when extra support is needed or crises hit. These things might be as simple as the fact that the boys who go on the skiing and sailing trips all come from the wealthier side of town and network with one another as they do so. More seriously, they could mean that when a crisis like death, disease, drug abuse, or divorce comes along, there is little else to fall back on in a working-class community other than your family, your neighbours, and yourself.

Back in the 1960s, James W. B. Douglas continued to follow his sample of children born in 1946 into secondary school. His next book, *All Our Future*, described the patterns of inequality that then existed in British secondary education. A big concern at the time was what was called *wastage* of ability or talent amongst *bright* working-class pupils when many of them left school as soon as they could, at the statutory leaving age. James W. B. Douglas, J. M. Ross, and H. R. Simpson summarized their results like this:

> *The upper middle class pupils were two and half times as likely to stay on after the minimum leaving age as the lower manual working class pupils. . . . Part of these differences is explained by the higher measured ability of the upper middle class boys and girls, but even when groups of similar ability are compared, the upper middle class pupils were approximately twice as likely to stay on.*[127]

Examination results in the GCE at age sixteen showed similar patterns. A good certificate—passes in four subjects or more—was twice as likely amongst the upper-middle-class students compared to their lower-manual-working-class counterparts. At this point, even at similar levels of high ability, when teachers were asked whether pupils were suited to higher education, they answered positively for 91 per cent of upper-middle-class pupils but only for 69 per cent of their manual-working-class peers. Ninety-three per cent of upper-middle-class mothers wanted their sons and daughters to progress to higher education, but only 59 per cent of the mothers of lower-manual-working-class students did.

The findings in Douglas's book are no anachronism. If anything, the inequalities are worse. A 2015 report by the Sutton Trust found that more than one-third of boys who were in the top 10 per cent of achievement nationally at primary school, yet were also from disadvantaged homes, were underachieving in their examination results by age sixteen. This "missing talent" was especially evident in former manufacturing towns and depressed coastal communities that make up eight out of ten of the poorest-performing local authorities in England.[128]

In *Our Kids*, a 2015 study of educational inequality and social-class division in modern America, Robert Putnam, the author of the bestselling book *Bowling Alone*, compares working-class and middle-class families who each have teenagers who have developed drug addictions. The middle-class families work closely with the schools. They purchase lawyers and counsellors, find outstanding rehab facilities, and build networks of support that get their youngsters clean again. Working-class families—always busy, often separated, and constantly poor, however—have none of these things, and their teenagers find it much harder to get help and recover. Class inequalities persist and are exacerbated over time when social supports in housing, health, and other aspects of public life start to fall away.[129]

Likewise, with the exception of the indispensable financial support provided by welfare benefits, my mum's nervous breakdown and other associated illnesses had to be dealt with by my family and me. This has been the case over the ages when working-class children have had to step up to take care of struggling family members. I missed many classes. If I wanted any spending money at all for a night out, a new shirt, or a trip to the football game, I had to earn it all myself with part-time jobs in the evenings and summer jobs as well. At one time, I worked two evenings and all Saturday on a market stall, cleaned a neighbour's car on a Sunday, and took a tray of bread and pastries every morning from the bakery to a local store.

I wanted to keep up a life with my mates in my neighbourhood too—so I didn't have to sacrifice my neighbourhood friends for those at school—so I would go out playing football and cricket with them after school, then come back home to start my homework around ten or eleven, after everyone else had gone to bed and I had the house to myself. If you get through all this, it can and sometimes does make you very resilient to many things that life throws at you later. Indeed, a classic study by Marvin Eisenstadt, made famous by Malcolm Gladwell, has shown that a disproportionately high number of children who lose a parent at an early age become very successful when they are adults.[130] It is as if these young people say to themselves at the time, "Well, if I could handle *this*, nothing else can be quite so bad."

But we can't just rely on individuals to be resilient. Schools have to help them be resilient too. When schools reach out to help the families whose lives have such an immense impact on their children, and work with communities to nurture the whole development of the young person, the results in educational achievement and well-being consistently improve.

There have been countless efforts to make secondary or high schools more responsive in this way. After the establishment of the World Health Organization (WHO) in 1948, for example, counsellors were introduced into U.S. high schools to provide career guidance and respond to psychological problems that adolescents were experiencing. But by 1963, studies revealed that counsellors were so few in number and consequently had so many students on their caseload that the whole system quickly turned into a vast impersonal bureaucracy.[131] And when austerity hits system budgets, as it did after the 2007 global economic collapse, some states regard counsellors as dispensable luxuries who can be amongst the first to be let go.

From the 1960s, state schools in the United Kingdom, meanwhile, adapted a solution from the elite private-school sector of houses, a bit like U.S. college fraternities or sororities. They appointed housemasters and housemistresses and year, or grade, tutors as part of a system of pastoral care for students' more personal needs. But state secondary schools were typically much larger than those in the private sector, so the pastoral system in state schools frequently became detached from the subject departments of the academic system. The two systems operated in separate silos, each with its own staff, curriculum, or timetable slots. Indeed, pastoral care staff at the state secondary schools often ended up dealing with problems caused by the academic system, such as insensitive teachers, uninteresting curriculum, and boring classes, that they had no power to remedy.[132]

Other moves have made secondary schools more like communities that develop senses of belonging, rather than bureaucracies that box students and their teachers into different subject departments. The Bill & Melinda Gates Foundation, for example, invested heavily in converting big high schools into smaller ones, and though stellar changes occurred in a few schools, elsewhere, the reorganizations into minischools or subschools were contrived and the results proved disappointing.[133] England, meanwhile, has a long alternative tradition of *village colleges*, or community schools, reaching back before the 1960s. These schools are open all hours to students and other community members, and they bring libraries and leisure facilities, along with adult classes, all onto one site. Others extend this community connection to the curriculum. For instance, Bosworth Academy—in the county of Leicestershire, where some of these colleges first started—has taken learning beyond the school gates and into the local community. It has fostered interdisciplinary inquiry into local historical issues such as the impact of the Norman Conquest on the surrounding area, and understanding the English Civil War through visits to sites like the Bosworth battlefields and the Richard III Visitor Centre. It has created ethical partnerships with local employers by running preapprenticeship qualifications for year 12 engineering students. The school has also supported local charities and helped to save the village public library from closure—a national issue—by working closely with the community and staffing it with volunteers.[134]

In the United States, there is the promising growth of what are known as *wraparound schools*. For example, my Boston College colleague Mary Walsh and her team have slowly and sustainably built a network of more than thirty schools that are "designed to help high-poverty, urban schools address students' nonacademic barriers to learning."[135] The model, which outperforms schools with similar student compositions, revolves around "a full-time School Site Coordinator (SSC) in each school . . . who connects students to a customized set of services through collaboration with families, teachers, school staff, and community agencies."[136] The SSC meets at the beginning of the school year with each teacher to develop a customized plan for each student. This connects students to community services and opportunities that can support and enrich them and then tracks, monitors, and follows up on their progress electronically. An ensuing Individual Student Review (ISR), led by the SSC, then brings together a broad professional team of psychologists, nurses, community staff, and educators to study and support each student.

Educating the whole child should not just be a priority for teachers of younger students. The early years of adolescence in secondary schools are ones where many students fall through the cracks between teachers and subjects.[137] For young people whose lives are filled with the distractions and disruptions that come from poverty and inequality, as well as from intolerance and prejudice, understanding and addressing all their development, not just their academic performance, is imperative. If we want to improve secondary school outcomes and narrow the gaps between rich and poor, we cannot expect individual teachers to shoulder the entire burden by themselves. It takes the whole school to support the whole child—teachers working with other teachers to support all students' success.[138]

In my secondary school years, I learned and survived by trial and error, with a mixture of problem solving, support from my grandma, northern grit, and more than a bit of sheer luck. Many other young people from homes in poverty didn't survive or succeed and still don't. There is no reason for them to struggle anymore.

CHAPTER 5
Worlds Apart

They hate you if you're clever, and they despise a fool.

—John Lennon

In the 1960s, while I was at secondary school, two sociologists from the North of England, Brian Jackson and Dennis Marsden, undertook an unusual yet hugely influential study. Instead of investigating what happened to the working-class failures in education, to those who had been left behind, they chose to study people like themselves—working-class students who passed the eleven-plus, made it to grammar school, and then moved on. What distinguished the working-class students who were successful from the ones who were not, and what lasting impact did this have on them, their lives, and their careers?

In their classic book, *Education and the Working Class*, Jackson and Marsden took a sample of ninety boys and girls, including themselves, from Huddersfield in Yorkshire (the *Express*'s absolute worst town in England by its recent standards![139]) who had passed the eleven-plus and gone to grammar school.[140] They then tracked these students through into adulthood. Who were these upwardly mobile boys and girls? What kinds of families did they come from? How did they cope with being lifted beyond their own class—above and away from their families and their friends? And how did this affect them when they took up careers in later life?

Presidents and prime ministers who have been upwardly mobile often make a big deal of their own education and of how similar versions of it could do a lot for others like them.[141] Both Margaret Thatcher, the grocer's daughter, and Theresa May, the parson's child, extolled the virtues of the grammar schools that had done so well for them. Barack Obama, the son of a single white mother and an estranged black father, was the recipient of a scholarship to an old private school that lifted him above and apart from the circumstances that disadvantaged many of his peers. So why, his administration thought, couldn't charter schools do the same for other minority students with ambition and talent?

This is why Jackson and Marsden's questions about working-class students who had received a selective education are so powerful even today for all those who experience upward mobility through education. Many competing answers were and are plausible. Do these students become intellectual ambassadors for their class and its interests? Do they become defiant opponents of ruling-class oppression? Are they what the Italian Marxist Antonio Gramsci called *organic intellectuals* who remain connected to their roots—teachers, politicians, media specialists, and academics who will be champions of social justice and equality in society?[142] Or will they move out of their class, away from their parents and neighbours, and become absorbed into a conventional and conservative culture of elitism and individual success? Then again, will they become angry, frustrated, and alienated women and men, belonging to neither one world nor the other yet cynical about both of them?

Jackson and Marsden's study paralleled my own education as a working-class schoolboy, and when I read it at university, its findings had more than purely intellectual significance for me. What had happened to their students, and what was happening to me?

Two findings of Jackson and Marsden's research stood out and still do.

1. Many successful working-class children are not truly working class at all. They are actually *sunken middle class.*[143] They are the children of families who for some reason have lost standing or status and are eager for their children to get it back.
2. Academically successful working-class children find themselves increasingly torn between two cultures—the academic culture and middle-class networks of their school on the one hand and the working-class culture of their neighbourhood friends on the other. They devise different ways to manage this cultural disparity.

How have these explanations compared with my own lived experience of being educated, and how do they still matter in the 21st century?

Sunken Middle Class?

The Hargreaves family always saw itself as working class. My granddad fitted gas cookers. We had come from generations of weavers. Mum had worked in factories and cleaned people's houses. My uncles and brothers had all worked in factories too. We'd lived in a rented council house and only got our own home through winning a competition in the newspaper. Money was always tight, and after my dad died, we ended up on welfare. My university costs were financially covered by a local council grant, as was my school uniform.

I was an upwardly mobile working-class kid. I passed the eleven-plus test fair and square. We didn't even have an indoor toilet or a bay window like most of my friends, but here I was in the top stream in the best boys' school: a testament to the postwar push for equal opportunities provided by the state.

In contrast to all this, though, my dad had gone to grammar school and had been prevented from going to university only because his family couldn't afford it. Although his mum had worked in industry, his own dad had been a small tradesman who made mill workers' clogs. My father was a dispensing chemist and then a manager for the small warehouse of the local pharmaceutical chain. I helped him with his paperwork. Unlike Jackson and Marsden's families, where many middle-class women had married down because of the death and the dearth of men from the war, my mum married up. My dad wasn't well paid, we did struggle for money, and after he died, we fell on very hard times. But we were a family with aspirations, expectations, and hopes for the future, including through education. We were quintessential examples of what Jackson and Marsden called the *sunken middle class*. Have too many of us—candidates for high political office especially—made exaggerated claims about how humble our beginnings were in order to validate the American Dream and its global equivalents?

When Jackson and Marsden entered the homes of their sample who had fathers with manual-working-class jobs, they concluded that "these were all manual workers' homes; yet manifestly this did not always fit either with the bountiful display of material possessions, or with their whole style of living."[144] Six of the fathers had turned to manual work after their businesses had collapsed. Twenty-five families had a middle-class grandfather on one side of the family or the other, and the parents in question (the sons and daughters of these grandfathers) had come down in the world compared to their brothers or sisters, the families' aunts and uncles, who now advised on the children's education. Having become the "poor relations" in these families, they kept a distance from their working-class neighbours around them so they would not be dragged down any further. In essence, Jackson and Marsden concluded, these families—one-third of the sample—were "submerged wings of middle-class families thrusting their way upwards through free education."[145] Grammar schools, in other words, provided a counterfeit kind of social mobility that did not open avenues for the "true" working class at all:

> *One of the consequences of throwing open grammar school education has been that middle-class families who have collapsed through ill-health, bankruptcy, foolishness or any of the stray chances of life, have been able to educate their children out of their fallen condition and reclaim the social position of their parents and grandparents.*[146]

The issue of education overclaiming its benefits for social mobility and equity persists. Do schools that claim to perform above expectations with working-class or minority students do this with students from a whole range of working-class or otherwise disadvantaged homes? Or do they get to take their pick from working-class or minority families who, for one reason or another, like Jackson and Marsden's, are highly motivated to choose a particular school, sign contracts that will ensure they monitor attendance and homework, and generally express an active interest in their children's education?

Especially in the semiprivate world of charter schools in the United States and academies in England, heroic turnarounds in school performance in poor communities often depend on selecting students by lotteries from motivated parents who have chosen to enter those lotteries; on accepting students only when their parents agree to supervise their progress and ensure compliance with school requirements; on rejecting students who have severe learning disabilities or language difficulties; or on *off-rolling*, or pushing out, students who aren't making the grade before the tests are taken and the results start to show up.

The children and young people who attend these schools may be working-class or minority students on paper. But for those who don't get into these schools, their parents may be too ground down by poverty or too busy earning a meagre living working multiple jobs on zero-hour contracts to make choices, gather information, or enter lotteries. The parents may be in prison, on drugs, or in another country. Teenagers may be living on the street or in cars without any adult supervision at all. Exaggerated claims by many charter schools and academies about how they transform working-class lives may therefore still apply mainly to those working-class families who are more aspirational, or in which the children may be looked after by a lone parent, devoted grandparent, or diligent aunt or uncle who is able to push them despite the family's limited financial resources, or the death or departure of one parent. Or these families may comprise refugee parents who took a step down into manual work or low-level service jobs in their receiving countries when emigration made them leave their former, higher-status professions behind. These kinds of immigrant parents are often highly ambitious for their children's education in the nations that have taken them in. The upward mobility of these atypical groups and their schools is too readily used to chastise the remaining public schools for poor performance with misleadingly similar students when these schools have no philanthropic funding and still have to take any and all students whom choice and selection have left behind.

Grammar schools create a system. Charter schools do too. These are systems of rejection of the many, as well as acceptance of the few. The disadvantaged groups who are given the chance to do well through selective examinations or with semiprivate interventions may not be as desperately impoverished as the rest. Selecting a few who already have some things working in their favour is not the same as offering equity and mobility to everyone.

At the same time, especially for those children who exist on the edge of poverty, whose families have suffered a major blow, who have fled from war-torn countries, and who want to succeed despite the considerable obstacles in front of them, the *sunken middle class* or *submerged middle class* seems an unkind term, a churlish pejorative.

The concept suggests not a dignified desire for higher learning and a better life but a desperate and sordid scramble to retain and restore social standing, security, and privilege that is driven by what the American sociologist C. Wright Mills once called a sense of *status panic*.[147]

How does all this apply to my own case? When I was fifteen, I'd passed my exams, and, because we were struggling for money, our extended family pressured my mum and me into having me leave school to get a clerical job in a bank. I'd been educated. We needed the money. Other than my dad, I'd progressed further in school than any family member ever. So shouldn't I make a sacrifice and look after Mum, since she and my dad had looked after me? There were blazing rows with my granddad, but I was insistent I should head on to university. Once more, my brave mum fought her dad—the dad who had opposed her marriage—and stood by me.

In this respect, the relationship between the so-called sunken middle class and their educational success is not necessarily or only a privilege—or a given. It's a process and a struggle. Not to recognize the efforts of families and children who succeed in the face of great adversity does them a considerable disservice. The upwardly mobile elements of the working class have to endure enough condescension from privately educated elites for being nothing more than industrious little "oiks" or "swots," without also having to be subjected by left-leaning intellectuals to the insinuation that they were never truly disadvantaged, are still the beneficiaries of white privilege, or did not have to struggle to succeed at all.

Two Cultures

Many years ago, my son, Stuart, who is now a law professor, made an astute comment to me. It was meant as a compliment. "The problem with you, Dad, is that you're too smart for ordinary people and too ordinary for intellectuals," he said. He was spot on.

For much of my life, I have lived within and between two worlds, two different ways of being. Having spent a couple of hours getting along famously with my mother, uncles, cousins, and old neighbourhood friends, the subject would often eventually change to something like immigration, and suddenly we would be worlds apart. They tried to insist I didn't have to live near the people they did, while I pointed out why their prejudices were wrong. It was a dialogue of the deaf. Voices rose, arguments got heated, and eventually we had to find a way to change the subject back to something else.

Amongst academics and with other elites, my life has had other kinds of awkward moments. I sometimes find myself making unfamiliar references to popular culture or throwing in an out-of-place swear word or two in formal meetings or presentations. I might fail to show appropriate deference to a dignitary or simply fall short in the routines and rituals of introductions and other niceties at cocktail receptions where I'm more likely to get engrossed in a conversation with one of the waiting staff instead of courting a potential donor. I once greeted the former U.K. education minister David Blunkett, who is blind, with the words "Nice to see you," for example. My wife, Pauline, puts this down to my tendencies to blurt out the very words that least need to be said at a particular moment. But whether that is true, I do often feel awkward about what to say to someone in authority when diplomacy and decorum are called for instead.

I came by all this honestly when I started to make the long daily trek out of my neighbourhood to grammar school on the other side of town. I had two sets of friends now. I did different things with them. And I put a lot of effort into ensuring they never met.

With my mates in the neighbourhood, I played football and cricket up the park several times a week and did my homework long into the night after I got home. When I was still only fourteen and fifteen, I organized marathon trainspotting trips for my mates and me across multiple towns and cities to visit engine sheds where old locomotives could still be found in the dying days of steam. And I went to the football games on Saturdays to stand on the terraces, before the days of hooliganism, with the rest of the working class.

At school, I hung around a lot with my friends there, especially Jack and Jim, who, on the ladder of parents' social class, were a rung or two up from me (and my friends in the neighbourhood). In a forerunning version of the movie *Wayne's World*, we went to Jack's house on Saturday nights to listen to the sounds of Eric Clapton and Cream, the Beach Boys' *Pet Sounds*, or Van Morrison's *Astral Weeks* coming through Jack's woofers and tweeters. We kept our own weekly handwritten pop-music charts and spent hours discussing, comparing, and arguing intensely over who'd made our top twenty that week—the Animals, the Who, or the Kinks; Procol Harum or Jefferson Airplane; and Otis Redding or the Supremes (who we once went to see perform at the Manchester Free Trade Hall), along with a few bizarre one-hit wonders like Whistling Jack Smith.

In the oncoming age of Monty Python, we also imitated our comedic heroes, like John Cleese, Michael Palin, and Eric Idle. We improvised rants and sketches that made us laugh until we couldn't stand up. I joined the local theatre, to take bit parts playing Shakespearean night watchmen, and then sneaked off to the local pub with the other players for my first experiences of underage drinking. We were more than a bit like the artsy characters in Jonathan Coe's *The Rotters' Club*, a novel set in a selective Birmingham secondary school in the 1970s.[148]

And it was this world, not the one in the neighbourhood, that started to welcome girls into my life. Suddenly, when I was sixteen, I gained newfound confidence after finally having my two front teeth crowned—they'd been broken in a bicycle accident when I was nine years old. I was Toothy no more. To my friends' amazement, I enjoyed an on-again, off-again relationship with a gorgeous Catholic schoolgirl from Burnley. We even saved up for, planned, and completed a 270-mile hike together for three weeks over Easter, up the then barely walked Pennine Way, the backbone of England, from hostel to hostel, through rain, mist, and snow.

Many of these interests of mine and of others like me were not part of the grammar school curriculum. My passion for hiking across bleak northern moors or watching my football team on a Saturday afternoon was not something my secondary education overtly valued. It promoted golf, sailing, rugby union, and ski trips instead. Pop and rock music were profane compared to classical music or even jazz. When I picked the book I would be awarded for the school's English Reading Prize—Alfred Wainwright's step-by-step guide *Pennine Way Companion*[149]—I was ashamed to show it to anyone, as it didn't seem to be the kind of culturally appropriate literature my prize was supposed to merit. Now it sits proudly on my shelves of travel and adventure books, a battered bundle of partially dissolved pages that was my stalwart companion for almost three hundred rain-soaked miles. There were huge parts of my life that brought me great fulfilment but that had little or nothing to do with school. As far as possible, I didn't really want my official school life and my out-of-school life to cross paths at all.

Most of Jackson and Marsden's students were also trying to find ways to navigate between the two very different worlds of school and home. They'd keep their accents at home but soften or drop them at school—code switching as they moved between one and the other. The grammar school was not all of a piece, and, both on their own as well as with subcultures made up of particular kinds of friends, students responded in different ways.

The orthodox, conforming student "belonged to two worlds" and "sometimes developed two identities to match." "I had this feeling of not belonging anywhere," one of the girls said.[150] Others coped differently. I was more like one of what Jackson and Marsden described as a "tight mesh" of "refusers" who were "*within* but *against* the school." They valued school*work* but not school *life*, with its institutional rituals and symbols. Like me, they "recoiled against common images of 'dominance' or 'leadership': school uniform, teachers' gowns, prefects, the Honours Board, the First Eleven, the Scout Troop, the School Corps, Speech Day, Morning Assembly, Expected Public Decorum."[151]

Then, and to this day, I disliked academic, religious, and military uniforms and regalia, the symbols of hierarchy, dominance, conformity, regimentation, cults, and sects. I know that my students value graduation ceremonies and the moment of status passage that they represent, and this is why I have participated dutifully in graduation ceremonies as a professor, but as I have sat in the front row, wearing my medals, as is expected for an endowed chair, I have felt mainly discomfort and estrangement.

At school, I found a way to avoid morning assembly for months by wandering the corridors and explaining to passing teachers that I was looking for boys who were avoiding assembly! I regarded the Scouts as little more than a paramilitary organization. I rarely wore proper uniform, partly because I couldn't afford it but also because I didn't agree with it either. When my performances at cricket during PE classes merited selection for the First Eleven, I showed up wearing nothing resembling proper kit and was never asked to play again. Though I was a good tennis player and reached the semifinals of the school cup against boys two or three years my senior, I couldn't afford and didn't really want normal tennis gear, so I was never invited to play for the school team. Sport was something I did with my mates, not for my school.

This was now my way of being. Work hard, do well, show initiative, use unconventional methods if you want to or have to, but don't buy into the old school tie. If you buy into one thing, you're often selling out of something else.

Cultural Capital

I was in a grammar school, and the Norwood Report had said my type of mind was supposed to be interested in "learning for its own sake" and building a "coherent body of knowledge."[152] But the knowledge and the ways of acquiring it were not neutral or timeless. They exuded and expressed what French sociologist Pierre Bourdieu called *cultural capital*—ways of knowing and being, distinction and taste, that are acquired and presumed in ingrained and unspoken ways in the life, culture, and curriculum of schools and other organizations.[153] Succeeding in schools, especially more elite schools, often requires conformity to and effortless mastery of the knowledge and life that make up those institutions and the privileged classes who most benefit from them. Ease with ritual, team spirit, adeptness at literary or cultural allusions, musical and artistic taste—these are the sorts of elements that make up the cultural capital of academic schools or elite universities, that middle-class families already often possess, and that many working-class students find alien and hard to acquire.

The best way for me to demonstrate this process in action is to fast-forward more than fifteen years. My most extreme experience of elitist cultural capital and its exclusionary nature actually occurred after school and university, when I went on to be a lecturer at Oxford University in the early 1980s. I gained many things of value from my five years there—team teaching with some of the most distinguished scholars in my field, learning how to work with mature graduate students who were experienced leaders in their schools, and engaging in positive partnerships with a dynamic local education authority led by Sir Tim Brighouse, future chancellor of schools for London. I also picked up the obscure skill of punting up and down the River Cherwell, which enabled me to entertain and impress friends and colleagues on conferences we attended together in Oxford for many years into the future.

As an academic coming down from the North and up from the working class, however, being an Oxford lecturer also required my participation in all kinds of arcane rituals that were both snobbish and surreal. Oxford University exuded privilege. It still does. Much of this is enshrined within its college system. Most scholars who joined the university faculty were appointed as members of a department, like classics or medicine, and also as members of a college where students and faculties across disciplines had rooms, dining rights, and other privileges. At that time, before the first competitive assessment exercise in the United Kingdom ranked universities and departments against one another, the field of education was regarded by the university as little more than a place to prepare its many graduates for teaching careers. The education department had very low status in the university, and only the most senior members of its faculty were awarded college fellowships. From time to time, though, the rest of us would get invitations from other faculty to join them at dinner.

Amongst other things, the college dining tradition was designed to promote conversation across fields and disciplines. You might find yourself seated next to an astrophysicist on your right and a medieval historian on your left one night, then sandwiched between a pure mathematician and a classicist on another. In fairness, this experience did train me with a lifelong ability to strike up a conversation with anybody, on almost any subject, anywhere. But in the short term it also led to some bizarre interchanges.

The English upper-class affectation of mixing up *r*'s and *w*'s, as well as *v*'s and *b*'s, created ample opportunities for misunderstandings. At one dinner, for example, I spent several minutes listening to a gastroenterologist describe her specialized interest in the great bowel shift before I realized she was actually a linguistic historian who was studying something in the history of the English language called the great vowel shift.

In another instance, a colleague came back from a dinner where he had overheard two fellows talking.

"I'm having a big problem with moles," one of them said, pronouncing *moles* more like *mowals*.

"A problem with what?" the other asked.

"Mowals—mowals," he replied, frustrated. "What do you think I should do?"

"Frankly, I'd shoot the buggers!"

"No, no, not moles—morals. *Mowals*," said the fellow, who turned out to be a moral philosopher, not a horticulturalist.

These kinds of incidents were nothing more than amusing or a bit embarrassing. But the whole ritual of dinner at high table amounted to far more than this. For one thing, it was *high* table. At the dinners I attended, fellows and their guests sat on a raised long table at the front, above the rows of many students. Wearing of academic gowns was compulsory, and on the most memorable occasion, procession into the dining hall occurred in self-organized alphabetical order—mercifully simple for me, as my host was also called Hargreaves. Standing behind our chairs on one side and in front of them on the other, at ninety degrees to the students, faculty then waited before they could be seated for one of the students to recite grace in Latin at lighting speed that was designed to outpace all previous efforts. The result, of course, was utterly incomprehensible, even in Latin.

Taking our seats, we faced place settings of silver service cutlery with wingspans that would put many modern aircraft to shame. Six or seven courses were served, each with its own perfectly matched fine wine. Meanwhile, the students ate standardized slop that would not have looked out of place at Harry Potter's Hogwarts' Great Hall.

At the end of dinner, a select group of invited guests was asked to join the master of the college in his quarters. Three crystal decanters were placed on the table in front of us, with sterling-silver labels around their stoppers. They were George III vintage, and the labels alone were worth a small fortune each. What would take place next was explained to us very carefully in advance. One decanter contained port, one had sherry, and the third was filled with Madeira—another fortified wine. Each would be passed around the group, once and no more.

The item that was taken out next was accompanied by no such explanation for most guests, but luckily my host had warned me. It was a small silver casket. It contained snuff. That's right—snuff! The nearest thing I'd ever seen compared to this was my grandad smoking packs of 20 Woodbines in front of the coal fire! Because I had been forewarned that snuff might indeed be offered, I knew that there would be no obligation to accept it. Unfortunately, another guest, who, like me, had an upbringing and a social circle that were devoid of any acquaintance with snuff, was given no such advice. After inhaling the alien substance with gusto, he then proceeded to expel the entire contents of his nasal passages over the other guests for several excruciating minutes.

So I passed on the snuff. The last offering would be much more straightforward, I thought. It was a simple bowl of fruit. I could not have been more wrong. I had already heard the story of a distinguished Marxist historian who had been considered for an academic position. After his formal interview, this young, brilliant, but unworldly scholar was subject to trial by dinner. The dessert consisted of a deconstructed pineapple, the pieces of which had been reassembled into the fruit's original shape. All the diners were issued with skewers to remove pieces of the pineapple in turn. The process was like a game of edible Jenga where the task was to extract your own piece without the whole thing collapsing. The innocent historian didn't know the secret sequence for removing chunks safely, of course, and when he inserted and removed his own skewer, the pineapple fell apart in front of everyone, along with his career prospects.

Alerted by this apocryphal tale, I watched my fellow guests remove their pieces of fruit from the bowl. Uncertain how they were supposed to be eaten, I avoided the obvious traps like the pomegranate and even the plums. At the back of the bowl, I spied a solitary banana, and I selected that for myself, confident I could not go wrong with it. But then, I was shocked to see each guest, irrespective of the fruit in question, take a small silver knife and fork and proceed to cut and consume his or her own item, piece by piece. In all my life, except at my grandma's, in a bowl with sugar and milk, I had never used cutlery to eat a banana before, but dutifully I now followed their lead. In hindsight, a better version of me would have seized the banana and boldly peeled it by hand, like a primitive primate.

At the end of the evening, my host asked me what I thought of the dinner. With considerable understatement, I reflected that it was "a bit formal." Well, he commented, a few years previously it had been more formal still. At the end of dinner, the women would retire into one room while the men would proceed to another, to converse over brandy and cigars.

Elitist rituals such as these are intended to exclude as much as include, to make those in the know feel familiar and comfortable, while outsiders and the uninitiated will feel awkward, inferior, and intimidated. My wife, Pauline, and I lived in a tiny modern row house with two toddlers. Most of our meals consisted of fish fingers, or fish sticks, cheese on toast, and jelly and ice cream. On the rare occasions we had wine, it came out of a box, not a bottle. We had no foreign holidays, spent our weekends doing activities with our children, and had an occasional drink at the local pub or social club. Against this, the ritualized cultural capital of Oxford University was not only unfamiliar but, given our own beliefs and background, also offensive. In fact, when my wife accompanied me to a college dinner, it made her physically sick—a literal, as well as figurative, demonstration of her inverse disgust about all she was being subjected to.

Every so often, Oxford and Cambridge Universities wring their hands about becoming more accessible to students who have humble beginnings and have been educated in state schools. They'll advertise more aggressively and inclusively, partner more closely with schools in challenging circumstances, and invite groups of students from working-class communities onto campus to get a taste of college life. But what they won't do is change the culture, or the cultural capital, that they are trying to open up to more young people in the first place.

Back in school, more than a decade before the extremes of Oxford University, I was experiencing the effects of cultural capital in other ways. I had come very close to failing my advanced-level history exam and received a low grade that was insufficient for me to get into university on the first attempt. The syllabus had been made up of kings and queens, popes and generals, Pitt the Elder and Pitt the Younger, in what was a history of the ruling classes. It meant very little to me, given the background I came from. But in repeating the course, I would now have a new teacher, so things would surely improve—or so I thought. However, when our new teacher strode into her first class, the blackboard notes for the lesson were exactly the same as they had been for the previous teacher. I knew that unless I took my learning into my own hands, I would be doomed.

So off I went to the reference room of the public library to consult old examination papers. To my delight, I found that every paper included exactly three questions—the number we were required to answer in total—on the social and economic history of agricultural enclosures, the industrial revolution, and so on. This was a history of collectivities, not individuals, of whole social movements rather than the actions of elites. It was one I could identify with. My teachers did not teach these items, but they would be on the paper, and if

I studied them thoroughly, I figured I could probably pass with a respectable grade.

Every night, after school, I headed for the oak-panelled library. I didn't tell my teachers. I performed miserably in my class assignments, but they didn't count towards the final result, so there was no point in expending effort on them. A few months later, it was time for the final exam. "Turn over your papers," the invigilator said, and, like a miracle, there they were: three questions on social and economic history. I wrote copiously and then waited for the results to be announced in August. A-level results were written out by hand on the back of an index card for each student. A teacher was stationed in the school office to pass out the cards to the lines of anxious and expectant sixth formers whose whole futures in or out of higher education were about to be given to them. By coincidence, on this day, the teacher in question was none other than our history mistress.

I stood there while she held out the card in front of me, not yet showing me what was written on it. "I'm very pleased," she said. "But I don't understand it." She repeated herself, unable to fathom the vast disparity between the wretched quality of my essays throughout the year on subjects I had not prepared for, and in which I had no interest, and my final examination result—the top mark—an A. I never told her my success had come from my studying an entire curriculum she had not taught us. But without the vocabulary to describe it, what I had, in effect, learned was that if you do not already have the cultural capital of the dominant elite and if you do not even want it, then individual effort, relentless application, and a counterintuitive or nonconforming strategy can get you a very long way. This was my own A-level equivalent of Tonya Harding's triple axel.

Gaffes and Gangs

One of the ways humour occurs is when things are brought together that are normally kept apart. The horse-racing commentary used as a voice-over for a golf tournament, the hapless fool who appears in the midst of a Shakespearean tragedy, the two sets of unalike in-laws who meet for the first time when their respective children are celebrating their engagement—these things are the stuff of farce and drama.

Jackson and Marsden report how the students they interviewed often found themselves being gauche or making gaffes at school events by not doing, saying, or wearing the correct or expected thing. Every so often, the worlds they worked so hard to keep apart would suddenly collide. This happened with me several times at school and continues to do so, from time to time, in life in general.

One of my biggest gaffes came at the end of what I now see as being a worthy effort on the part of my school to recognize my efforts and accomplishments when I was in the midst of family turmoil. I had entered myself for the English Reading Prize. This prize was a bit like a literary *X Factor*. In a series of elimination rounds, contestants had to read aloud, almost unseen, progressively more difficult passages from classical literature, onstage, to a panel of teacher judges.

I did not then have a great knowledge or even a working knowledge of English literature. Indeed, I was not even studying English literature (even though I wanted to) because English, an art, was forbidden as a subject combination with geography, then counted as a science, so I had to take my hated subject of mathematics instead. Yet for some unknown reason, although, unlike my brothers, I had never learned to play a musical instrument, I did and still do have an intuitive feel for the music of texts and words, and I can bring them alive in the way I say them. Even though I did not always fully understand what I was reading, I was somehow able to read it in a way that impressed the judges. Intriguingly, the British actor Christopher Eccleston, from a working-class home in Salford, recounts having had exactly the same experience when he performed readings at his first auditions.[154]

The judges had a long deliberation. Their decision was controversial. They would be awarding me the English Reading Prize even though I wasn't actually studying English. I'm sure I must have earned it, but in retrospect, they were very likely also giving a hard-working boy from a struggling family a break. And then they had the grace and decency to honour me twice more. They asked me to deliver a soliloquy from *Henry V* to a large audience at the town's arts festival. Seeing this as another form of drama and theatre, I donned a red velvet robe and black tights and gave an accomplished performance. They also invited me to give the vote of thanks to the upcoming visit of the Lancashire Youth Orchestra—a task normally reserved for the head boy. This time, I had no text, no script, and no idea what to do. It wasn't drama or theatre. It was institutional ceremony. I felt awkward and anxious as the rituals of cultural capital bore down on me. I didn't even *like* classical music. So I reverted to my everyday, nontheatrical northern accent instead.

"Ah'd like to thank thah Lancashire Yooth Orchestrah fur playin' fur us tooniiite," I said as I read from the roughly written notes in my trembling hand. It was a terrible let-down for everybody. The school had done its best for me, but its culture had ultimately collided with mine, and the result was not a pretty sight. I was never asked to represent the school again.

These cultural collisions were merely an embarrassment at my well-meaning school that wanted to lift me up but on the elitist terms that it and schools like it had defined. At home, I was headed for something far worse than just a bit of embarrassment, though. In my neighbourhood, as I hit sixteen, I was now practically the only youth left wearing a school uniform. My older brothers had left or were leaving home and were no longer there to protect me. I stuck out like a sore thumb.

In 1967, on FA Cup Final day (the English football equivalent of the Super Bowl), my brother Colin got married. The black-and-white photographs of the wedding show the happy couple surrounded by relatives from both sides of the family. Way back in the corner, almost out of view, sporting a big black eye, is me.

It had been coming for weeks. Though I was studying hard for my A-level examinations now, I still played out with my mates up the local park until it went dark—football in the winter, cricket in the summer. I was the only one in the neighbourhood not working full-time for a living and was suddenly a bit of a target. I could play sport as hard as anyone else, but I was a wiry kid and slightly built, and the people coming up the park now were not just my mates who wanted a game but also the local gang, who were looking for something else.

At first, there were taunts and jibes, even if I didn't know exactly what they meant. Only my ignorance protected me from their seriousness. There was and still is a washing powder in England known as Omo, and when they shouted I was an "Omo," I knew it wasn't flattering. But to be likened to a laundry detergent couldn't be that bad, it seemed to me. Of course, in broad Lancashire, without the *h*, *'omo* was short for *homosexual*. And their other favourite insult—*arse bandit*—was not, as I then thought, an accusation that I resembled an inept Mexican bandit riding a donkey in a cowboy movie either.

Over the course of a few weeks, there was a bit of pushing and shoving. Eggs were thrown at my bedroom window. Threats were issued in the street. Until one night, in the middle of a cricket game, one of the lesser members of the gang, lower down its pecking order, strode onto the field and came for me. We punched each other and rolled around on the floor. I got up, shocked to find myself covered in blood. It was his. I thought that would be the end of it now, but I could not have been more wrong.

Two weeks later, in the middle of a game of tennis, this time, the gang leader, a big bulky lad, walked onto the court, his entourage behind him. He had come specially dressed to fight as gang members did: black leather biker jacket, studded belt, and steel-capped pit boots. This was serious. I was petrified. I knew I could end up in hospital this time. He knocked my racket out of my hand and hit me bang in the eye. Unlike my brothers, I had and still have no fighting instincts, skills, or training. But my one-eyed body kicked into intuitive self-defence mode. Using a strategy that my tennis opponent later described as being like that of a demented windmill, I somehow managed to fight off my assailant as I rained down blows on his head.

He curled himself up like a shield, took a step or two back, then slowly began to remove his studded belt. I was wearing shorts and sandals and had not yet picked up any tips from Kirk Douglas or Russell Crowe on the finer arts of gladiatorial combat against a far-better-equipped opponent. All I had left were my words that I addressed not only to him but also to his gang behind him.

"What's the matter? Can't finish it off with your fists now, can you? You have to use *that* to beat me, do you?"

The truth was, he didn't. He could really have crushed me to a pulp just with his bare hands. But the hackneyed lines I'd probably picked up from an old black-and-white Western movie somewhere had done enough to hold him off and get him to think twice. After a few more insults were traded, he and his gang walked away. I don't know what happened to the gang after that, but I never had any trouble from them again.

We should never underestimate the power of words. They can be lifesavers. Teachers in tough secondary schools depend on this kind of verbal authority and agility all the time. In adulthood, on two different occasions, in Dublin and Boston, my using the right words in the right way at exactly the right moment has stopped men from beating women on the street and enabled the women to flee. Words talk people down from suicide attempts. They inspire others to greatness. They change people's minds. Actions speak louder through words.

The Meaning of Mobility

The lived experiences I have described are what often happen when there is serious inequality—when communities are separated, people no longer really know one another, and schools take out one social class from another or some members of a class or minority group from the rest. There is alienation and awkwardness, anger, envy, and resentment. Sometimes the dislocations and disparities cause outrage; sometimes a more diffuse sense of alienation and detachment; sometimes a kind of critical marginality that comes from being on the edges of both worlds—a bit in both but not completely part of either one.

The students in Jackson and Marsden's study had to endure accusations from neighbours and former primary school friends that they had turned into "stuck-up" snobs. Like my eldest brother, one of them even got assaulted when he was caught carrying his violin case to school.

The angst and estrangement of the working-class grammar school boy form a distinctive strand of thinly veiled autobiographies in English literature. D. H. Lawrence established the genre in his early works, where the protagonist, like himself, is the sunken-middle-class son of a woman who married down to a rough and violent coal miner.[155] Lawrence won a scholarship to the city grammar school, destined for a life as an artistic individualist, forever at odds with his origins.

In 1976, David Storey wrote a Booker Prize–winning novel with echoes of Lawrence in his account of another miner's boy, Saville, who goes to grammar school in the late 1930s. For Saville, "Between waking and sleeping was a continuous movement; rising, running for the bus, the hour long journey through the villages, the approach to the city, the walk to school, assembly, lessons, break-time, lunch."[156] After the long ride home on the bus:

> *He sometimes played in the field at the back of the house; the rest of the time he spent on homework. The village*

> *involved him less and less; it was more of an inconvenience, its distance and remoteness. He seldom saw his father.*[157]

Time passes. Saville leaves school, trains to be a teacher, and teaches miners' children. But he finds himself at loggerheads with the headmaster. His lover, somewhat older than him, summarizes his situation: "You don't really belong to anything," she says. "You're not really a teacher. You're not really anything. You don't really belong to any class, since you live with one class, respond like another and feel attachments to none."[158]

Acclaimed comedian and late-night U.S. talk-show host Trevor Noah knows how this looks when race is factored in. The illegally born son of a black Xhosa mother and a white Swiss German father, in apartheid-era South Africa, Noah was already destined to be an equivalent of the sunken middle class.[159] After apartheid eased and ended, Noah found himself in the A stream of a government school where there was just a handful of white students, even though the B-stream students who he encountered in the yard were largely black. "The white kids I'd met that morning went in one direction, the black kids went in another direction, and I was left standing in the middle, totally confused," he recalls.[160] How did Noah cope with all this? In the end, he experienced and expressed his marginality not in the sad and self-flagellating way of David Storey's Saville but through the comedy, irony, and parody of "an outsider." "I wasn't popular, but I wasn't an outcast," he explains. "I was everywhere with everybody, and at the same time I was all by myself."[161] In time, Noah turned these tools of negotiation and survival of the racially mixed and upwardly mobile into the political satire he uses to brilliant effect on his late-night talk show.

How do all these patterns of upward mobility play out in contemporary America? In his bestselling book, *Hillbilly Elegy*, self-avowed Republican J. D. Vance describes his own conflicted experiences of upward social mobility as he moved from Middletown, Ohio, on to Yale University.[162] Vance is empathetic about the decline of Middletown, where many of his family and their Kentucky Appalachian neighbours had moved in search of work. "Abandoned shops with broken windows line the heart of downtown."[163] At the front of the local theatre, he explains, is a big sign with missing letters. Like many other former industrial towns, including ones that have had songs and stories written about them by artists like Bruce Springsteen and Richard Russo, Middletown has become a metaphorical assortment of consonants with its vowels ripped out. How does Vance feel about all this, now that he has left? On the one hand, he looks back on the culture as a mixed bag. "Hillbilly culture at the time (and maybe now)," he writes, "blended a robust sense of honor, devotion to family, and bizarre sexism into a sometimes explosive mix."[164] But he also has contempt for how "people gamed the welfare system," lining up at the supermarket to buy soda pop with food stamps, only to resell it for cash that was then spent on cigarettes and beer.[165]

Raised by his grandmother, Vance psychologically splits his working-class culture of origin into the deserving and less deserving—the *respectables* and the *roughs* of British social reformers I described earlier.[166] His grandparents "embodied one type: old-fashioned, quietly faithful, self-reliant, hardworking." His mother "and the entire neighborhood embodied another: consumerist, isolated, angry, distrustful." Vance concludes with "I always straddled these two worlds."[167] Vance is like the upwardly mobile conformists of Jackson and Marsden's study—grateful for having had a source of positive influence in his life yet also a bit sanctimonious about his own sense of personal responsibility compared to the irresponsibility of much of the culture he left behind. In the end, he can't help getting preachy about the tendency of hillbilly culture to blow any money on trucks and big-screen TVs. "Thrift is inimical" as a way of life. It's culture that's the problem, Vance is telling us, not poverty.[168]

Life in the Margins

So there are many ways that the upwardly mobile sunken middle classes adapt to and explain the difference between themselves and those they've left behind. Some, like Prime Ministers Thatcher and May, along with a section of Jackson and Marsden's sample, commit and conform to the elite that embraces them. Others, like Storey's and Lawrence's characters, wander and drift through life without any clear purpose. Then there are those—another group in the Jackson and Marsden study, and Vance as well—who look back in anger and exasperation along with bitterness and disgust at those who, it seems, lived for the moment, made bad choices, and wasted their lives. Meanwhile, Trevor Noah's quick wits and quick feet equipped him with the humour to move in and out of different groups and see the funny side of all of them until satire enabled him to turn these tools against the abusers of political power.

How did I respond? I'd been sunken middle class. My struggles were real. I lived two lives, worlds apart, in both and in neither together. Like Noah, I was starting to develop some rudimentary talents in performance and in comedy—and I could run very fast when I had to as well. I could be in no groups or in many. I still can. Look at photos of me in groups, even with government ministers and the like, and unless people have made me take centre spot as the group leader, you'll usually find me in the frame, but far off to one side. In Jackson and Marsden's terms, I might have been able to achieve *within* my school, but I was also, in many ways, *against* what it stood for.

In my secondary school years, I was hardworking, creative, critical, and ironic—and more than a bit awkward (in both senses) and headstrong at times. I was not one of the really cool people in grammar school but not a loner or an outcast either. I'd not joined any political parties or marched for any causes. I rarely was, and still rarely am, a joiner. Like Ruth Bader Ginsburg—the "Notorious

RBG"—the octogenarian U.S. Supreme Court justice, instead of waving banners and joining in protests and parades, I try to use my professional skills and platform as a writer and speaker and on social media to argue and advocate for things that matter in the ways where I feel I can do most good.[169]

Being marginal or "out of place," in the words of the late Palestinian intellectual Edward Said, is not altogether a bad thing. It can be a source of great insight about things others have missed.[170] Not everyone can or should be jolly hockey sticks, or gung-ho, for the group. Being different, quirky, ironic, or simply quiet should be seen as an asset in a school culture, not as a threat to it.

At the same time, strong cultures should not create outcasts who are troubled loners with no sense of belonging. They should not make young people choose between their schools and their local communities, between the class and the gang—giving up one so they can succeed in the other. Schools should inspect their own cultures and curricula to ensure they embrace different languages, accents, and ways of being successful so they don't marginalize key groups of students. A curriculum that embraces and engages with popular music, social history, and contemporary literature—and not just classical music, the histories of elites, and traditional literary canons—shouldn't just be available to younger students, recent immigrants, and students in lower streams or tracks to get them going or keep them occupied. It should be a crucial part of how the curriculum and academic success are defined for everyone, including those reaching the selection point for university. Disadvantaged students don't just need more support in order to access elite cultural capital. The cultural capital defined by elites has to become more accessible too.

Social mobility for me was like a cultural maze as well as a social ladder—a maze tilted vertically, in fact. Eventually, I somehow found a path through it in ways that have helped others and myself. Like

Edward Said, I have benefited from being inside and outside at the same time. I have been able to become a bit of a public intellectual in my field where I can provide independent commentary on issues of the day as they affect the most disadvantaged or vulnerable groups in society. Although, from my grammar school perspective, the prospects of this would still be a long way in the future, I was fortunate to find or choose this path that has eluded many others. Many of these others, faced with my secondary school situation, aren't just marginal. They are marginalized. They are outcasts rather than outsiders. The price of abandoning their families, friends, accents, and communities for other cultures altogether is too high for them—and it is one they should never have to pay.

As for myself, as I hit eighteen years old and was coming to the end of my schooling, I still needed an intellectual and moral framework to give my inchoate and ironic insights some meaning, purpose, and direction. For all that, I would need to go to university.

CHAPTER 6

Higher Loves

Think about it; there must be higher love . . .

Without it, life is wasted time.

—Steve Winwood

I'd known for a long time I wanted to go to university. But I had no idea which one. The application process involved filling in a form for the Universities Central Council on Admissions—known as UCCA for short. The task was to pick six universities you wanted to go to and put them in rank order. You included your examination details at age sixteen and also listed any hobbies. By the time I applied second time around—I had not succeeded the first time—I also had a couple of school prizes to my name in English reading and geography. I loved geography and still do. On travels across the world, I can bore my companions rigid with minilectures on the geomorphological synclines, anticlines, drumlins, and eskers that surround us. I had already passed geography with an A grade, as well as an additional Special paper, an even higher standard of examination, that involved applying geographical knowledge to unfamiliar problems. I had a lot to build on, it seemed.

Like Jackson and Marsden's upwardly mobile working-class students, however, I blundered my way through the whole admissions process. I wanted to study geography but don't recall any teacher sitting down with me to discuss which were the best universities or where the best courses were. A small group of boys from wealthier homes in and around the town were being coached for their Oxford and Cambridge entrance exams, but I was never invited to join them. I didn't consult my family at all, as they had no knowledge or experience of universities or even the cities they were in. So Jim and Jack and a few other friends and I circulated bits of knowledge, hearsay, and gossip amongst one another about the best places to go and the ones to avoid.

I didn't want to be too close to home. If I felt lonely, I reasoned, I'd be too tempted to rush back. So I drew an imaginary forty-mile total-exclusion zone around my hometown, ruling out Manchester and Liverpool as I did so. I also didn't want to go down south to unfamiliar culture and country. This eliminated anywhere below Birmingham. In the end, I picked five universities and hastily added the London School of Economics, as I'd once visited my girlfriend in London for the weekend after she had moved there to go to Teacher Training College.

Fortunately, only one university—Hull—decided to interview me. I dreaded them asking me about my hobbies. An ivory-tower equivalent of an urban myth was about the student who went for an interview and wrote under "hobbies" that he played the violin (even though he didn't), at which point the interviewing tutor whipped out an instrument from behind his chair and demanded the student give him a tune! I stared at the empty box under hobbies, unable to think of a single interest I could mention. I didn't count my 270-mile hiking adventure that I had planned, paid for, and executed; my intense love and copious knowledge of rock music; my assiduously pursued pastimes of trainspotting and stamp collecting that I had now abandoned; or the hours I spent playing football and cricket in my neighbourhood. These didn't seem to be the sorts of things that universities regarded as hobbies. All I could think of was the instruments I didn't play, the teams I wasn't on, and the books I'd never read. In the end, I listed the default hobby of the time—reading. This gave my interviewer little to go on, and I stumbled my way into a rejection. Fortunately, other universities on the list never invited me for an interview, and so, uninfluenced by my maladroit self, two of them gave me very good offers instead.

The prestigious London School of Economics—the LSE—presented a requirement of a single B grade that I could easily meet. Here, in one of the top social-science institutions in the world, all my future networks and alumni were waiting for me—policy advisers, media specialists, ministers of state, on a global scale. Surely, this was an offer I couldn't possibly refuse. But I did. I never considered that one purpose of university was to establish lifelong networks. I'd only been to London once. The university was in the middle of a lockout as part of a student demonstration. It also wasn't long after the Grosvenor Square protests outside the U.S. embassy against the Vietnam War. Not only did London seem far away. But because I had no money to fall back on, and despite my own antiwar sympathies, it also seemed to be a place where continuing disruption could mean I might never get an education at all.

So the choice was Sheffield, in Yorkshire—a place I'd never been to, at a university I didn't know but that still offered some reassurance of being in the North. Sheffield, it turned out, had the world's most innovative geography programme, but this was not what occupied my mind in my first year there. The 1960s were still in their swing, and I wanted to be part of them.

Getting Too Silly

Eventually, over four years at university, I would start to develop a way of understanding and committing to greater *equality* on behalf of my class, to draw on my own experiences of social mobility to learn how to become an advocate and even an activist for young people who are disadvantaged and marginalized, by building a career in education. But mainly, my being a social-science student, and then becoming a teacher, was initially driven more by the spirit of the 1960s in Britain and its preoccupation with freedom, liberty, and libertarianism as a reaction to arbitrary authority within unresponsive institutions. Sometimes this libertarian orientation was intellectually and professionally responsible. But, for a while, at least, it was less serious than that and often even downright silly.

Within hours of arriving in Sheffield, I met my roommate, Bob, the son of a miner's widow from the Northeast. He had long jet-black hair and a badass moustache and played the guitar like a maestro. This was the coolest guy I'd ever known. We bantered back and forth like we'd known each other all our lives, then headed into town to meet mates of his in a quickly expanding circle.

Freshers week, the first week, was wild. We built an amphibious raft out of an old bookcase, trolley wheels, and oil drums to enter the university boat race and careen down the filthy, rubbish-festooned River Don. It was a northern parody of the Oxford and Cambridge toffs' equivalent. Then there was the beer marathon—six pubs in three miles. I finished the race proudly, not because I was in the lead but because I was the first one not to do projectile vomiting before we got back to the students' union building. There were rock concerts, pyjama parties, and lots of drinking. While American students were smoking dope and dropping acid, the lower age for legal consumption of alcohol turned many British students to the more easily available and comparatively innocuous alternatives of beer, wine, cheap cider, and fake champagne. I wouldn't recommend this now, of course, but this was just how it was—away from my small-town home, money to spend, lots of very cool friends, and nobody to account to for my actions.

I grew my hair long, way past my chin. On the sides of my face, I sprouted enormous curly muttonchop sideburns—or Mungo Jerries, as we called them, after a pop band that pioneered the style. I picked up outfits from second-hand stores—an old navy officer's jacket and a Royal Air Force greatcoat with brass buttons—and wore them in a ragamuffin style that showed no respect for their origins at all. When I came home for Christmas, my mum was mortified by my appearance. Looking back, I now feel shame and regret about all the sacrifices she had made just to see her son and all the others make a mockery of all that many of her generation had given their lives for.

A group of six of us moved into an old terraced house together, on a dead-end street called the Nook. We started a folk-rock band—the Nook Band—in a style that was a cross between the more modern bands Barenaked Ladies and Mumford and Sons. Two members of the group had real guitar-playing talent. I painted up an old washboard, acquired some thimbles, attached a bicycle bell, and wrote and sang some of the songs.

Our first efforts were calamitous. We knocked our instruments over, and some of us fell off the stage. But they asked us back, and we became fun to watch. Then we practised and got better, creating four-part harmonies, opening for bigger acts, and touring folk clubs around the city. After performing before one of Britain's legendary folk-rock artists, John Martyn, in the university's refectory, its largest venue, we were offered contracts to cut demos. Then the lead guitarist's girlfriend took up with the second guitarist, and that was the end of that!

At the start of all this, I found a new girlfriend. In some ways she was my polar opposite. She came from the South, while I was from the North. Her family was wealthy, and she had a very posh accent. In contrast to my socialism, she was politically conservative. She had been captain of her school's lawn-tennis team, while I had never even seen a grass tennis court, other than watching Wimbledon on black-and-white TV. I was intrigued by the differences even though we existed in a 1960s counterculture bubble where differences didn't seem to matter.

Fashionably turned out in miniskirts and makeup, with her hair tied up in bunches, she was Mary Quant in a Jimi Hendrix world. She was as daft as I was, with a long string of quick quips and a surreal sense of humour that bounced off my own. Together, especially in company, we could banter back and forth, improv-style, for hours on end. I don't remember a lot of intellectual conversation. For the most part, we were just outrageously silly. We were antiestablishment but, unlike our U.S. counterparts, without the Vietnam War to justify it. With our friends, we watched and learned to recite, off by heart, now legendary Monty Python TV sketches such as "The Spanish Inquisition" ("*Nobody* expects the Spanish Inquisition"), "The Dead Parrot Sketch" ("The Norwegian Blue *prefers* kipping on its back!"), and "Is This the Right Room for an Argument?" ("I've told you once!").[171] It was all great fun and a little bit wild. Like the sex.

We were not the first postwar generation to go to university with public money. Before us came the duffel-coat brigade—the serious-minded students described so well in David Lodge's *How Far Can You Go?* who tried to square newfound independence with worries about getting pregnant and guilt about religion.[172] But we left home just as the contraceptive pill became widely available, and this cast our inhibitions to the wind. My girlfriend revelled in the naughtiness of sexual activity in the university lounge, the library—just about anywhere at all—and I gladly went along with it. Sex was a recreational activity within a relationship, part of all the fun, not yet an expression of lifelong love and affection.

University for many people was and sometimes still is not only about academic study but about being independent, away from home, doing things without your parents watching, becoming responsible after being irresponsible, and finding out who you are and can be all over again. It still should be that for many young people. But it can't all be about sex, drink, and rock and roll (for most of us, there never were any drugs). Eventually, you have to come to terms with the fact that you are at a university, not a holiday camp or the School of Rock!

Step by step, a sense of reality imposed itself. Halfway through the year, I looked at my bank account and realized I'd already spent three-quarters of my grant. That put an end to most of the drinking. As the first-year exams came closer, it became clear I hadn't been studying much or even going to many classes, so I put in a lot of cramming in the last few weeks and managed to scrape through. Then in the first summer, coming back from a hitchhiking jaunt in a futile search for vacation jobs, I got my girlfriend and me stranded on a motorway bypass at four in the morning in pouring rain. She was not impressed. Neither were her parents. Since texting had not yet been invented, she subsequently used the Royal Mail to notify me that I'd been dumped. It seemed my own little summer of love had gone a bit too far, much like the spirit of the decade itself. The 1960s were transitioning into the 1970s. Purple haze would soon give way to brown and beige. Years of counterculture and consumerism were about to be followed by escalating unemployment, coal strikes, power cuts, and winters of discontent. Life in Britain was starting to get less silly and a lot more serious.

First Love

In October 1970, I returned to Sheffield to discover two higher loves. My mates and I living at 12 the Nook were second-year students now. It was time not to go to other people's parties but to throw our own. We brewed our own beer in a big plastic waste bin. Fellow students brought bottles of Hirondelle Red, Blue Nun Liebfraumilch, and cheap QC sherry. What more could we British equivalents of frat boys have wanted?

Pauline Beales came with a group of a half dozen girls she had started sharing a house with. They knew I was no longer spoken for, as we used to say. I first saw her by the kitchen door. She looked lovely in a Joni Mitchell kind of way—a bit alternative, but not too much, with a maroon maxiskirt that gave her a sinuous appearance, and natural good looks that spoke for themselves. In the more intimate parts of our life, maroon is still our colour of choice.

Blonde hair, parted in the middle, fell about her shoulders. From her petite standpoint, she had a way of looking up that exuded kindness and modesty with just a hint of invitation, and a lovely, unaffected smile that drew me close. She made me nervous, so I put my arm against the door and talked nineteen to the dozen in case she should think about getting away. Eventually, when I had to step out for a few minutes, I passed her my plastic cup of cheap white wine and asked her to look after it for me, assuring her I'd be back shortly. That, she has said many times since, is when she knew she had me. Or was it the other way round? Either way, this was the understated start of a fifty-year love affair.

I didn't ask her out the next night, figuring she might already have another date lined up. So we arranged to meet the day after that. From that moment on, we became inseparable. Too close for our own good, my eldest brother would often say. Wrongly. She'd grown up on a council estate in Leyland, another northern town, famous for its paints and buses, and just a few miles up the line from the railway station where Paul Simon wrote "Homeward Bound." Pauline had studied hard to get to where she was. Her subjects were Latin and ancient history. She detested the militaristic prose of Caesar's *Gallic Wars*, where soldiers were forever getting in and out of trenches, but she loved the erotic poems of Catullus and read out modern, raunchy translations of them to me. We made up jokes about the past pluperfect and the ablative absolute. We listened to Cat Stevens and Joni Mitchell on my old red Grundig tape recorder that I'd bought second-hand for eight pounds when I was still at school. After only a few weeks, we made love, for that's what it was—tentatively at first, but better and better as we grew closer together, in my room with wall coverings I'd made from stapled psychedelic wrapping paper.

Pauline was smart in ways and on subjects different from mine, and she had a contrasting temperament too. She fasted on the streets to raise money for Oxfam. She wanted to work for Voluntary Service Overseas. She was not politically ideological. She just wanted to help people who had less than what we had. In the words of Cat Stevens, she was my "hard-headed woman" who would "make me do my best."[173] Inspired by her, I did a bit of photography for the university community action group in poor parts of the city and volunteered once a week to visit an elderly working-class couple in a high-rise flat.

My new girlfriend was clever and witty yet also practical and sensible. Shy in some ways, she knew how to stick up for herself in others, particularly with me. I asked my family what they thought of her. "A lot better than the last one," they declared.

Pauline didn't like me getting *too* silly, but she appreciated moments like the time I collected her for dinner and danced up and down the stairs impersonating Fred Astaire in *Top Hat.* Ultimately, we moved into her bedsit together, and I learned what a resourceful cook she could be, even on a tiny Baby Belling stove, tucked into the corner. We were never lost for words—then or ever since. We could talk all day until the sun went down and far into the night. To our adult children's amusement, we still can.

In June of 1972—our last year as undergraduates—after exams were over, we hitchhiked up to the English Lake District for a short youth-hostelling holiday. On a perfect English summer's day, we stood at the end of a little boat landing by the side of Rydal Water—Pauline in a tight red sweater and me in a purple skinny-ribbed button-down item that was very much of its time. I got down on my knees. I was convinced I wanted to spend the rest of my life with her, I said, and asked her to marry me. I had no money and no ring to offer her, just myself. "Don't be silly," she responded. But this time, I wasn't being silly at all. She saw that in me now and graciously accepted.

Second Love

In a year or so, Pauline and I would be married. But for a long time to come, I would also have another love that would capture my heart and occupy my mind obsessively, almost every day. It was an intellectual discipline that a Frenchman called Auguste Comte introduced in the 1800s, referring to it as the *science of society*.[174] Its name was sociology. Respected by continental Europeans and their admiration for social thought, sociology in the 1970s was ridiculed by the British chattering classes who epitomized their distaste for it in an overused cartoon showing a roll of toilet paper with a sign at the side declaring "Sociology degrees—please take one!"

We took three subjects in the first year at Sheffield. I had chosen sociology as an unknown wild card. It intrigued me, so in the second year, I switched from geography to make it my sole major. In the coming years, I would build a library on theories of *symbolic interaction*—human meaning and identity in relation to issues like the development of the self, adolescent youth cultures, experiences of mental illness, and the stigmatization of people who are marginalized.[175] I now spent most of my spare cash on books rather than beer. These books would help me understand how we see ourselves and build our identities through a looking glass of other people's reactions to us, how people shape and are shaped by their circumstances, how they form cultures and subcultures of people like them, and how acts that seem strange to outsiders can make perfect sense to those within these cultures. The books pointed to how institutions like mental hospitals, boarding schools, and public bureaucracies posed threats to individual freedom, dignity, and identity. I was beginning to acquire some intellectual frameworks to make sense of the world and where I stood in it by filling up a shelf with little Penguin books.

Conversations with my friends now took a sharp intellectual turn and developed intensity as we engaged in vigorous arguments about miners' strikes, Northern Ireland, unemployment, students' rights, existentialism, Marxism, and the struggle for equality and social justice.

In my last year, I took a course on the sociology of education with an avuncular old figure in a baggy pinstriped suit and shiny black shoes. His name was Keith Kelsall. The founder of the sociology department, he was an expert on the demographics and statistical inequalities of education. Apart from our engagements with Jackson and Marsden's *Education and the Working Class*, though, much of the course passed me by. I knew well enough the extent of social-class inequality in Britain in and outside education by this time, and the numbers didn't add much more to that understanding.

Sitting before fewer than a dozen of us in his office every week, Professor Kelsall came across as a quiet, cautious, and conservative man. He seemed a lot like the senior civil servants he had studied in one of his projects. He never overclaimed anything and frequently used the word *propensity* to describe trends and tendencies rather than asserting categorical rights and wrongs. Then, suddenly, in our last two classes, it was as if the pinstriped carapace fell away from his portly frame, as a mischievous smile broke forth. Waving a bunch of small paperback books at us, he announced that an interesting group of writers had emerged on the education scene and that it might be worthwhile for us to look at them together. They were known as the *deschoolers*—a group of writers who promoted the disestablishment of schooling as we knew it.

I rushed out to buy all these books with their rebellious and anarchic ideas. Neil Postman and Charles Weingartner set out an argument in 1969 on how to turn teaching into a subversive activity and told their readers and their students to get out their *crap detectors* to identify all that was manifestly wrong with schools and society.[176] In the 1967 book *Death at an Early Age*, a young Jonathan Kozol gave harrowing accounts of the injustices inflicted on African American students in the schools of Boston.[177] In 1968, in his now timeless classic *Pedagogy of the Oppressed*, Brazilian educator Paulo Freire promoted the virtues of liberation pedagogy against prevailing models of *banking education* that treated learners as vaults in which deposits were made.[178] We were also introduced to the thoughts of an obscure Croatian Austrian philosopher and Catholic priest, Ivan Illich.[179] Twenty years before the internet, in the 1970 book *Deschooling Society*, Illich argued that we should disestablish schools altogether and replace them with networks of conviviality where people with shared interests but differences in expertise could seek one another out to undertake teaching and learning together.

I devoured all these texts voraciously, excited and animated by their radical, antiauthoritarian approach. Paradoxically, although the books argued for the end of schools as we knew them, they incited me to want to work in education for a career. The most insightful and intriguing amongst them, by far, were two books written by the least flamboyant of all these writers—a U.S. teacher and educational adviser who had previously served on submarines. His name was John Holt.

Holt would eventually become a poster child for the libertarian homeschooling movement, but his earliest books, *How Children Fail* and *How Children Learn*, for which he collected classroom observation notes in the late 1950s and early 1960s, were compellingly simple efforts to understand why so many primary school students failed in school and why they adopted a vast range of bizarre, self-defeating strategies just to fake the appearance of learning. Holt's books offered me what then felt like profound insights into the most basic and prosaic interactions between teachers and students in school and how damaging they could easily be. They exerted an enormous influence on me.

In *How Children Fail*, Holt begins boldly, "Most children in school fail. For a great many, this failure is avowed and absolute. Forty percent of those who begin high school drop out before they finish."[180]

He continues:

> *But there is a more important sense in which almost all children fail: except for a handful, who may or may not be good students, they fail to develop more than a tiny part of the tremendous capacity for learning, understanding and creating with which they were born and of which they made full use during the first two years of their lives.*[181]

"Why do they fail?" he asks rhetorically.

"Because they are afraid, bored and confused."

Schools and teachers, Holt goes on, are obsessed with right answers, and students spend hour after hour being not merely anxious about but afraid of getting the wrong answer. "Most children in school are answer-centered rather than problem-centered," Holt writes.[182] "They see a problem as a kind of announcement that, far off in some mysterious *Answerland*, there is an answer, which they are supposed to go and find out."[183]

This explains a range of otherwise strange but common student behaviours. They wave their hands in the air amongst a crowd—but not too conspicuously, secretly hoping they won't be called on. They whisper and mumble their answers knowing that their teachers are "tuned to the right answer, ready to hear it, eager to hear it," even if it sounds ambiguous.[184] Students just want to race on to the next question and answer and use "don't-look-back-it's-too-awful" approaches to avoid checking their work.[185] Then there's "Guess-and-look"—"start to say a word, all the while scrutinizing the teacher's face to see whether you are on the right track or not."[186]

Students are afraid of being wrong, desperate to please their teachers, and eager to avoid mistakes at all costs. "These self-limiting and self-defeating strategies are dictated above all by fear," Holt asserts. "Most children in school are scared most of the time, many of them very scared. . . . The adjustments most children make to their fears are almost wholly bad, destructive of their intelligence and capacity."[187]

Holt understands all too well the teacher's dilemma of working in a system like this:

> *I try to use a minimum of controls and pressures. Still, the work must be done—mustn't it?—and there must be some limits to what they can be allowed to do in class, and the methods I use for getting the work done and controlling the behavior rest ultimately on fear, fear of getting in wrong with me, or the school, or their parents.*[188]

The result, Holt seems to be saying, is that students and schools distort their effort and activity into creating the *appearance* of learning rather than actual learning. In lines that could have been written about test-based competition amongst 21st century schools, Holt describes how the schools encourage it:

> *Our standing among other teachers, or of our school among other schools, depends on how much our students seem to know; not on how much they really know, or how effectively they can use what they know, or whether they can use it at all.*[189]

I was good at getting the right answers myself when I was at school, but not in everything. For example, I couldn't swim until well into my twenties. As a child, I dreaded swimming classes. Our physical-education teacher, an abrasive Scotsman whom we unimaginatively nicknamed "Jock," had an uncomplicated approach to swimming instruction. He stood bowlegged on the balcony overlooking the pool, with his arms folded. "Swim! Swim!" he bellowed.

How do you produce an acceptable response when it's palpably obvious you can't swim? A small group of us in this unenviable position took a protracted time getting changed into our swimming trunks, or we misbehaved to get thrown out of the pool, or we concocted bogus reasons in forged letters from our parents, for missing swimming altogether. But, most cynically of all, we would walk across the shallow end and back, stooping down so just our heads remained above the water. We created the *appearance* of swimming. Sadly, provided we created the appearance of swimming, our teacher was prepared to accept it.

This is what life is still like for too many students in the 21st century. Not just once a week, but most of the time, they encounter test items they do not understand, content that has to be rushed through to get to the end of the course, or material that is unfamiliar and intimidating. So they use all the strategies Holt describes and more—misbehaving, being absent, losing or forgetting their equipment, trying to borrow pencils from other students who don't have them, and just fudging and faking their efforts to create some appearance of learning whenever they can. Even some supporters of standardized testing concede that many students, especially younger students, experience anxiety when they have to take high-stakes tests and that things must be done to mitigate this.[190] Holt shows us that the problem runs even deeper than this. The basic problem is not just a bit of anxiety amongst especially sensitive students. It's fear.

Higher Purpose

When I graduated, it was 1972. The 1960s were over. Pauline and I were both twenty-one. Suddenly, we felt older. We had pledged to be married, to spend our lives together. We had made a commitment and started to feel the call of responsibility. Pauline wouldn't take up her department's offer to study for a master's degree. We would both become teachers. Sociology hadn't led me to march in protest against anything, to convert to Marxism, or to become a champion of the working class—at least not yet. But starting to master this complex discipline had begun to give me a framework for understanding myself and where I was in the world. It had also helped me grasp the ways other people struggled to find meaning and purpose in institutions that oddly—and, sometimes, infuriatingly—appeared to discourage these things. Children were amongst these people, and I thought, as an educator, I might be able to help them. My lived experience of social mobility was starting to transform into some kind of mission.

A few years later, when I applied to do educational research, my social-psychology professor wrote that although my ideas were sometimes disjointed, I had progressed a lot by the end of my course and was showing signs of thinking independently. The university had done most of what it was supposed to do. It had given me the space to be silly and the time to get over it. It had not provided me with future networks of awesome alumni. But it had offered me the chance and responsibility to take charge of my own destiny, away from the oversight of my family, and to find intimacy and then love in my life.

Sheffield University had introduced me to disciplines of thought and understanding, motivated me to compile my own library, helped me find a vocation, and started to equip me to work in a profession. It had provided me with a liberal education. In time, this foundation would help me build my understanding, create my own frameworks, and become clearer about not just what I was fighting against as a libertarian but what and who was worth fighting for in terms of social justice too. And on the way, I'd been in a band, developed a decent repertoire of pool and snooker shots, and fallen in love. In 1972, when unemployment in the United Kingdom had doubled in just over five years, if you came from a modest home and didn't want to go back and live with your parents, this was about as good as it got.[191]

CHAPTER 7
The Full Monty

No one said anything to me about the full monty!

—Horse, in *The Full Monty*

Sheffield is the location for one of the most successful movies of the 1990s. *The Full Monty* is the story of six men who have been made unemployed when the city of steel collapses and manufacturing jobs move overseas. Eventually, these men of many shapes and sizes decide to take off all their clothes—"the full monty," in northern parlance—and form themselves into a group of striptease performers.[192]

In one of the scenes, the character played by actor Robert Carlyle collects his son from an old Victorian primary school in a working-class part of the city. This location, now a boxing club, is just a stone's throw from an almost identical building where I undertook my main teaching practice when I trained to be a primary school teacher.

I had actually started applying for postgraduate training programmes in geography teaching in the middle of 1972, as there were only a handful of teaching jobs in sociology. At my first interview, I received the sterling advice that with only a minor qualification in the subject, although I would probably pick up a job, I would find it hard to progress later on. Would I consider primary school teaching instead, I was asked. And so, while Pauline trained to teach Latin in the university-preparation programme, I went down the hill to the college of education to prepare to teach primary school. I had no idea whether I'd be any good at it.

The *full monty* is about more than just taking all your clothes off. More generically, it means "the most or best that you can have, do, get, or achieve, or all that you want or need."[193] Learning to teach is definitely the full monty. As an undergraduate student in social sciences, I could go to some classes and miss others, have a slow start and then cram it all in at the end, and get up late without really commencing studying or going to lectures until midmorning. Unless you are grossly irresponsible, though, there is no option to have this in-and-out, on-and-off existence in teacher training. Once you are out in schools, other people—young people—depend on you. There's no more choice of getting up when you like and staying in bed when you don't, or of not turning up if you are feeling tired, hungover, or a bit ill. Suddenly, raw as you are, the students need you. And you have to be there for them. It was all or nothing now: the full monty.

Experience Counts

One of the reasons I chose the education profession was that I wanted to go into teacher training at some point. I'd witnessed and experienced truly inspiring teaching at the end of primary school. I knew, in a deep way, the power that great teachers have to liberate students, set them free in their explorations, and lift them up to reach heights they scarcely thought were possible. Then in secondary school, I had encountered the evil twin of great primary teaching. This teaching was at best a mediocre trudge through uninteresting content. At its worst it was execrable.

So when my grammar school sent me a follow-up questionnaire in 1972, three years after I had left, asking me about my future aspirations, I replied, with more than a touch of bitterness and spite, that I wanted to go into teaching and then teacher education to prepare a generation of teachers who would be far superior to the one that had taught me. Some people go into teaching because of magnificent teachers who inspired them. Others want to right the wrongs inflicted by teachers who made their education a protracted experience of unnecessary suffering. I went into education for both reasons.

University- and college-based teacher preparation has many critics, not least those who have experienced it directly. George Bernard Shaw, the playwright with more than a few Fascist affiliations, famously remarked that those who can't do, teach.[194] If he had added that those who can't teach, teach teachers, he would have found many supporters. Teacher education is notorious for the immense gap it creates between theory and practice.

The classic criticism of generations of student teachers has been that the educational theories learned in university courses don't work in practice. Looking back, new teachers have usually said that they learned a lot from their practical experience in school but not much of value from their coursework. Back then, college courses employed "methods" teachers to teach reading, mathematics, and other subjects. There were also sociologists who seemed to devote most of their time to identifying what was wrong with schools and teachers. This was a bit dispiriting for those who were joining the profession for the first time. Psychologists made sense to those who worked with children as individuals or in small groups, but their insights and recommendations didn't seem to apply to whole classes. And what philosophers had to say seemed to have little bearing on classroom life at all. Amidst all of this, nobody seemed to devote any deliberate time to help trainee teachers with the thing that worried them the most—student behaviour and classroom management.

Teachers who look back on their training and complain that the courses were idealistic and irrelevant have usually been more ready to acknowledge the value of practical experience in schools. It was here that aspiring teachers confronted the realities of classroom life and where experienced veterans took them under their wing and taught them the tricks of the trade and, sometimes, a few of its dark arts (don't smile until Christmas, severely punish the best-behaved student early on as a warning to the rest, and so on) that didn't appear in their course materials or get covered in their essay assignments.

One line of argument about the uselessness of university- and college-based teacher education was that students came into teaching ready to transform the world but that the gap between theory and practice, and life in the school of hard knocks, made them conservative, turning them into cynical realists. However, a study by British professor Colin Lacey found that most students who entered teacher training were already quite conservative to begin with but pretended to hold more radical views in order to pass their coursework with their liberally minded professors.[195] Once the coursework was out of the way, the demands of the existing school system enabled them to revert to their original standpoints.

Lacey's findings fit a period when, as Jackson and Marsden had found, many of the upwardly mobile working class looking for their first professional job drifted into teaching for the want of other options. Even for me, although my motivations to be a teacher were genuine and real, like many other upwardly mobile young people, teaching and social work were the only two professional jobs I knew directly. I'd no idea what it meant to be a doctor, lawyer, or architect. Teaching for many of the others who were upwardly mobile wasn't merely familiar. It closed the circle of being good at schoolwork. It wasn't necessarily the fulfilment of a radical ambition to transform lives or promote greater social justice. Before the proliferation of law degrees, teaching was the qualification to get so you would have something to fall back on if other things didn't work out.

Class Returns

People in many professions like medicine, social work, or the military will sometimes talk about early experiences that were transformative for them—when they were pushed onto the front line, confronted enormous challenges, or were faced with overwhelming need and then found something in themselves that they didn't know was there. This is *not* what happened to me, at least not at first.

At Sheffield, there were two periods of teaching practice. The first was four weeks, towards the end of the first term or semester. I was placed on a council estate that was reputedly one of the best. In a city that was becoming racially diverse, my class was completely white. There were some challenges, but in the main, the families to which these children belonged were overwhelmingly *respectable* rather than *rough*. They were model tenants who worked hard, looked after their gardens, and ensured their children attended school.

I was given a class of top juniors, aged around eleven years old. After a week or two watching and helping, I took over the class for most of the time. Apart from one lesson when a flock of migrating birds distracted the entire class in the middle of my being observed and evaluated—I suspended the lesson and took the students to the window to discuss migration—nothing out of the ordinary occurred. I made various attempts to initiate groupwork and inquiry and, having been inspired by the early movements for environmental education and community studies, figured out how to use the nearby tower block of council flats that most people thought were a big blight as a learning resource instead. I took the students to the top of one of the blocks so they could look down on their estate, identify landmarks, and draw sketch maps of what they had seen. This got them into the basic idea of maps, mapping, measurement, and space that we returned to in the classroom.

This first teaching practice seemed to me interesting enough, and I tried a number of new things with varying degrees of success and failure. When my supervisor from the college concluded her observations, she wrote that I would turn out to be either a brilliant teacher or a terrible one. There would be nothing in between, she said.

What subsequently made the difference for me was developing a stronger sense of meaning and purpose. I hadn't discovered this overwhelming sense of purpose on my first teaching practice. I had not yet been challenged enough. Like the proverbial curate's egg, I was only good in parts. Being brilliant or terrible was equally likely. Beyond the anarchic impulse to overturn the culture of right answers and defend children against adult and institutional tyranny, I was still to discover the sense of moral purpose that would anchor as well as animate my efforts.

My second teaching practice—two months long—hit me with a sense of purpose like a ten-ton truck. The practice got off to a shaky start. There were two of us in the programme who, as young men, were still sporting rebelliously long hair. By an uncanny coincidence, we found that our teaching-practice placements were in the same school—he on the first practice, me on the second! The dilapidated school was in a highly impoverished part of Rotherham, a small steel town on the edge of Sheffield that in 2018 the *Express* judged to be the second-worst town in England.[196] In educational terms, though, Rotherham has also been made famous by Dolly Parton, who brought her children's literacy initiative to it from the United States.

Before I headed out on teaching practice, my college peer warned me that the headmaster was an ex-military type who had made him get a haircut. So I took myself off to the barbershop, and the hair that had fallen down to my shoulders was taken up as far as my chin. Nonetheless, after I'd been in the school for just two or three days, the head called me into his office and demanded I get a haircut. I explained that I had been informed about his policy so had already got one. This seemed more than reasonable to me. He was not impressed, though, and insisted I go back to get another one. I dug in my heels and refused. We were at an impasse.

All my life I have been resistant to the imposition of arbitrary judgements by top-down autocratic leadership. For a long time, this was almost always male leadership. This kind of defiance was a deep-rooted part of my class and culture. I was already aware of and reacted strongly to any hint of unfairness and injustice in primary school, including the curious incident of the school bell at playtime. At secondary school, I had been within the school but also against it. By the time adolescence rolled around and I had no father to fight, I battled with my strict Victorian grandfather instead. In one memorable argument, he shouted out, "You *will* always have the bloody last word, won't you?" At this point, my grandma calmly intervened by observing, "Well, a chip off the old block then, isn't he?" It was the only time I ever saw my granddad speechless.

When it came to friction with unwanted and unwarranted authority, my social-class upbringing definitely informed it. The generational conflicts and counterculture of the late 1960s certainly fuelled it. But until I developed greater self-awareness, fighting the ghost of my dead father very probably inflamed it. With much of the aggravation that autocratic male leaders got from me, they deserved a lot of what they got. Most of them were hierarchical, manipulative, self-serving, and, like narcissistic dads with up-and-coming sons, even directly competitive.

But looking back, I see there were also times when I flew off the handle too quickly, should have had more empathy for their point of view, and might have cut them a bit of slack. Even so, with figures like these who represented the dominant pattern of male leadership, I developed no desire to be an organizational leader myself for years, and even decades, to come. These were not the leaders I wanted to be. It was only when leadership changed, became more inclusive and benefitted from more women and a younger generation of men becoming part of it who demonstrated how to lead differently, that I too began to develop the inclination to step forward on behalf of others.

Back in the college of education, my second teaching practice had now stalled. To their credit, my college lecturers negotiated another placement in an equally challenging school in a poor part of the city—the neighbourhood next to the location for *The Full Monty*—and after a reassuring interview with its head teacher, I made a start. The school was very diverse, or, as it was expressed in the language of the day, multicultural in nature. I should have known I was in for a hard time when the first face to greet me enthusiastically outside the school gates was that of the naughtiest boy from my first teaching practice. He had moved across town in the interim to live with his dad instead of his mum. Although he was a bit of a lad, when I left the previous school, he had nonetheless given me one of my most moving Christmas presents ever: a pair of his dad's used socks, wrapped up in newspaper, that, he insisted, had been worn only once.

The rule of thumb for beginning teachers was that students would watch what you did for a few days and then start to test you out. Unfortunately, my class hadn't read the manual. The kids didn't even give me a few minutes. The moment I was alone with them, I had to field multiple requests to go to the toilet. One of the liveliest boys in the class threw himself across the floor from one side to the other. I was shocked. I would have to put my foot down and assert my authority, of course. But, I realized, I would also need to engage them so much with their learning that they would sometimes forget about misbehaving.

Now it really was time to dig deep, draw on everything I had, and find other parts of me I didn't even know were there. Some of this was about sheer survival, of course. But it was also patently obvious that many of these students were in great need. Although I had experienced struggles in my own family upbringing, they were nothing like the difficulties that these students who stared back at me every day encountered. Despite their teacher's best efforts, the standard of work was a long way below what I had seen in my previous school. Many of the students found it hard to concentrate and were easily distracted. Each day as I observed the students in their shabby clothes and with their wan faces, the signs of poverty were everywhere. Social class was back on my radar in an unavoidable way.

My supervising teacher was the opposite of the one on my previous practice—enthusiastic, organized, encouraging, forgiving, and full of strategies and ideas. Before very long, she felt confident enough to let me have the class all to myself for the majority of the time. Being a good teacher was no longer a matter of making learning interesting or boring, of succeeding or failing at the job. It was now a matter of making a difference to children who were on the wrong end of class inequality, and this was something I now felt driven to do.

Like all idealistic new teachers then and now who have found their sense of purpose, I worked all hours of the day and night to come up with projects, activities, and strategies that would help them to be successful. I designed lessons, differentiated activities, drew enormous posters for the classroom walls to brighten up their learning space, made work cards, and ran off endless worksheets on the school Banda machine. This was a strange apparatus with a cylinder full of ink, an intoxicatingly hallucinogenic fluid, and a handle at the side to crank out piles of problems and activities on sheets of shiny paper. I gave up evenings, weekends, social life, sex, and sleep, and after several weeks, I eventually had to take to my bed for a couple of days with what felt like flu but was really just plain exhaustion.

My effort and ingenuity could not be faulted. I had a passion to help these students learn and give their lives a lift, and from time to time I saw students who had been difficult or disengaged come to life with some of the experiences I was able to give them. But looking back, I realize that the passion I infused into their learning was a passion for the things *I* was interested in and enthusiastic about—such as transportation and children's TV programmes—not what they most needed or what was relevant to their cultures and identities.

A number of my students were of Caribbean heritage—or West Indians, as we called them at the time—but in the school and the college, no one ever taught us about how race, culture, language, and immigration were relevant to teaching, learning, and the curriculum. I knew how to try to get my students excited and engaged, but I understood nothing about their cultures and identities that would help me engage them more effectively. I was innovative, hardworking, deeply committed, and, by the judgement of my college and classroom supervisors, effective. But I was doing this work *for* my students, drawing on *my* enthusiasms and not on what was necessarily most relevant and important for them. I had a lot to learn. I just didn't know it yet.

To progress further as an educator, I would need more time, more experience of all kinds, and more knowledge about inequity and its relationship to the kind of knowledge that was built into and kept out of the school curriculum. I understood how students could be herded into a right-answer culture because of teachers' adult authority. Like Paulo Freire, I wanted to ditch the banking model of education.[197] What I still had to grasp was how all this was not only or mainly about insensitive teachers but about confronting a more deep-rooted approach to teaching and learning and the curriculum in schools that suited students from privileged families more than those whose parents or guardians were economically impoverished or culturally marginalized.

In 1973, these two sides of my work, life, and brain existed side by side. The neurons hadn't yet connected; the dots hadn't joined up. It would take time, experience, research insight, and practice across all the years, decades, and countries of residence that lay ahead. But in the meantime, there were some other dots to join up as well. It was time to get married.

No Horse and Carriage

A piece of my wife's family's folklore concerns the time I had to ask her dad's permission for her hand in marriage. Pauline's fourteen-year-old brother, Bob, the youngest of four girls and two boys, was hiding behind the couch. He remembers what happened to this day. Pauline's dad, a huge and fearsome bear of a man, was indulging an eccentric habit of his that involved lying on his back, in front of whoever was there, ostentatiously throwing pennies in the air and catching them. In the midst of this strange activity, I edged into the living room with my grovelling request. He was grudgingly gracious, but looking back, I know it couldn't have been easy for him.

Bill Beales, Pauline's father, was the son of a steam-locomotive driver. When he was a child, he had to share a bed with his dad, who was dying of throat cancer. At thirteen, he was required to leave school and go out to work, as his family couldn't afford any more education. He served in the army and took numerous evening classes in technical drawing and design so he could eventually become an aeronautics engineer for British Overseas Airways Corporation. After he and his wife raised their six children in a large council house out on an estate, his family was eventually able to move to a new development of private detached homes opposite the town's public park. Pauline was quite bookish and seemed to be the most successful academically. Her dad hoped that she would become a school headmistress one day. Had he lived long enough, he would have seen his dream come true.

So with my long-haired hippie appearance, Mungo Jerry sideburns, and awkward, not to say argumentative, social skills, I must have seemed like a disappointing choice, to say the least. When he first made a surprise visit and walked into the living room of the grubby terraced house at 12 the Nook that I was sharing with five other dishevelled young men, he was confronted with a giant poster of a familiar children's cartoon character, Rupert the Bear. Rupert, a wholesome teddy bear with checked trousers, featured regularly in one of Britain's most conservative newspapers, the *Daily Express.* But this was no ordinary Rupert poster. It was produced by a satirical 1960s' magazine, *Oz*, and showed everyone's favourite bear sporting a massive hirsute erection. This, along with an uncleaned home with congealed fat in the frying pans, led him to walk away complaining that I was nothing more than "a tramp who lived in a slum."

Unfortunately, he wasn't just referring to my student residence. When he visited my home in Accrington and discovered it was a terraced house on a cobbled street, to my mother's shame, he refused to get out of the car his wife was driving and accompany her inside. This behaviour seemed callous at the time. But he must have felt that after all the sacrifices he had made, his daughter, for whom he held out his highest hopes, was now taking a big step down. In time, as he saw us study and progress, and could see how we were together in the world, including with our newborn son, he would start to relent. But both his daughter and I were children of upward mobility. We were moving up and in together. Our finding each other shouldn't have been that much of a surprise to him.

On Bastille Day, July 14, 1973, Pauline and I were married in a small low-budget wedding that our families could barely afford, in the local Parish church. The ceremony was simple and lovely yet unremarkable. There was just one exception. To the vicar's visible disappointment, and years before Meghan Markle, Duchess of Sussex, would make it newsworthy, we broke the news to him that Pauline would not be taking the traditional vow of obedience. Honouring each other would be more than enough!

Following a small hotel reception, with no music or dancing, we had a brief honeymoon awaiting us in the Lake District, a free gift that came with booking the reception. The coach—Britain's equivalent of a Greyhound bus—was scheduled to leave from Preston Bus Station, ten miles away.

Love and marriage, supposedly, go together like a horse and carriage. But we couldn't afford a horse or a carriage at our wedding, or even a hired car, so my brother Colin agreed to drive us to the bus station instead. One of Colin's ways of supplementing his income was to buy old cars—bangers, basically—repair and renovate them as he was using them, then sell them on for a profit. We should have considered the risks of this when we accepted his offer of honeymoon transportation. We had already cut our timing very fine, but two miles into our journey, almost right outside the church where we had just married, his car spluttered to a halt. Our coach was still eight miles away. There were no taxis or cell phones. Time was running out. We were completely stranded!

Then, in the distance, a hundred yards or so ahead, we spied a local bus stop. We struggled out of the back of the car—me in my twenty-five-pound suit from Burton's, the tailor, Pauline in her long checked "going-away dress," both of us covered in confetti. We grabbed our suitcases from the car boot, not knowing whether we would catch the next bus and even less aware of all the things that were ahead of us in our lives.

We were unaware that within a year, we'd leave our new teaching jobs in the Midlands and head back up north, where I'd start my graduate work. We didn't know that Margaret Thatcher would assume power, jobs in higher education would disappear, and we'd have to move from city to city in a struggle to find one temporary post after another to try to stay in work. We didn't foresee that we'd have two children before we were twenty-seven because we would worry that time was moving on. We couldn't possibly have envisioned how, one day, we'd emigrate almost four thousand miles across the ocean to Canada.

Ahead of us, a bus pulled into the stop. We ran as fast as our improbable outfits would allow us, towards the steel pole on the rear platform. In the future, I would write or edit more than thirty books. There would be prizes, sales and impact, students and classes, school and district parterships, good and bad collaborations, meetings with ministers and prime ministers, and all of this with a B-list celebrity or two thrown in along the way. Before all of this, we would also worry about where the next jobs were coming from and how we would pay the bills. We'd count up every single item of expenditure at the end of each week in a little lined notebook to see where savings could be made. I'd also negotiate a pay rise when I asked my first boss in higher education to guess what we had for our meat roast at Sunday dinner and then explained that all we could afford was chicken livers.

At the age of twenty-six, I'd give my first big speech, without looking at my notes, to more than a hundred of the leading people in my field, all of them older than me, the day after our son was born. It was delivered in a blur, after thirty-six hours without sleep and after two celebratory pints of beer at lunchtime, just before I went on. And I'd get a standing ovation. In time, I'd learn to keynote confidently in front of thousands. I would also vomit repeatedly with anxiety before one of my very first invited international speeches—and collapse with exhaustion years later just before another, when my presentation about leadership succession, and how the leaving of leadership was a preparation for the leaving of life, felt too close for comfort.

The bus started to set off. We threw our cases inside and reached forward, grabbing the pole and each other as it pulled away from the stop, giving the other passengers a matrimonial sight they'd never forget. In the future, our children, born just thirteen months apart, would keep us awake night after night, week after week, until we took to separate beds so we could look after them and ourselves without collapsing. We would be so tired that we'd leave our three-month-old daughter in her pram at the meat counter before we remembered where we'd left her. We'd also bathe them together and read to them every night—Postman Pat, Roald Dahl, and twins Topsy and Tim, long before Peppa Pig came on the scene. We'd go out with them every weekend and holiday we could, pushing them in strollers down the length of the River Thames and along the Grand Union Canal, then walking around the coastal paths of Wales and Cornwall, through driving snow across England's Lakeland peaks, and up hundreds of miles of the Niagara Escarpment in Canada.

With passing years, our limbs would eventually begin to creak a bit. The TV would sound more and more muffled, and I'd blame it on newfangled production techniques! We are still well, thankfully, but none of that was ever planned far ahead or strategically certain either. When young scholars sometimes ask me, "How do I get and plan a career like yours?" there's no easy answer, other than "Do your job, with purpose, to the best of your ability, all the time, and seize your opportunities when they come." In our case, we just made most of it up as we went along, one rung at a time.

We arrived at Preston Bus Station just in time to get on the coach. Seated just behind the driver, with her new husband, was my old primary school playmate—the front half of God. She was heading off on honeymoon too. What a surprise! Many things in life surprise us. We cannot plan it all out in advance—though, with their crèches, camps, and courses, many of the existing elite try. In general, though, that's not how social mobility works for the rest. In career terms, the big things rarely come early or easily, especially for the likes of us—people without networks or alumni, without old money or wealthy families to fall back on, without the cultural capital that is always at hand for so many others. All of us will experience loss and disappointment. Many of us will experience fulfilment and accomplishment too. But, aside from the curses of racism and poverty, the things that will make the difference between how much there is of the first and the second, relatively speaking, are what your family teaches you and the kind of education you get.

At its best, public education gives everyone a chance, engages our existing and emerging interests, helps us find our sense of purpose in life, and connects all of this to our cultures and our lives, whatever our circumstances, however clumsy or gauche we might initially be. At its very best, public education gives us both mobility and continuity. There is the mobility of new opportunities and experiences, of more chances to be fulfilled and to make a contribution in the world. Public education at its best also conserves and preserves the best values we have grown up with, the cultures we are from, the languages and accents that define us, and the knowledge that connects to our lives. It doesn't ask us to move on up by leaving our selves behind.

People should be able to have economic and occupational mobility but also retain at least some degree of identification with the cultures and communities that raised them. An engaging curriculum that can connect with young people's existing lives while also connecting them to the lives and world of others, and a common school system that holds students and communities together rather than dividing them early by selection and choice, can provide the upwardly mobile generations of the future with both roots and wings.

There are many kinds of lives worth living, but an educator's life can help create all these possibilities for other people. For that reason alone, it is surely one of the best lives of all. A 2019 U.K. survey found that almost 30 per cent of young people feel that life has no purpose. Attract some of them into teaching, where they can benefit the lives of others, and that number may drop like a stone.[198]

Ahead of us, at the end of our coach ride—up in the Lake District, where I had first proposed—in an oak-beamed hotel room with a floral carpet and creaking floorboards, Pauline and I would experience, in every aspect of our being, the full monty with each other, not for the first time or the last, not just for one night or two, but for the rest of our lives. Unprepared but idealistic, completely unworldly, but hopefully not unworthy, we were, in the words of a country-music song, now two sparrows taking flight together into the hurricane of life.[199]

CHAPTER 8

The Bigger Picture

You cannot change what you are, only what you do.

—Philip Pullman

This final chapter is different from the rest of the book. It has no new autobiographical detail. Instead, it builds on clues arising from this memoir that point to the bigger picture of social mobility as a system. It connects more fully with the wider literature and evidence on social mobility. How does social mobility affect all of us? What do the possibilities for social mobility look like today? How can social mobility be increased, and how can people's experiences of it be improved? Or is social mobility the wrong answer to the right question of how we can have a fairer and more just society?

The chapter speaks not just to individuals or even schools about how they should strive for and manage mobility. Instead, drawing on this memoir, it also asks what the narratives, hopes, and dreams of other ordinary or "common" people who want a decent and fair chance in life imply for social policy. It addresses the responsibilities that governments, all parts of the public, and members of the wider society have to increase equity and equality of opportunity, through strategies of social mobility and other strategies too. It uses my voice to connect with the voices of other people who come from communities like mine and from other backgrounds of disadvantage. It asks how those who already have advantages and privileges can support progressive social policies that promote mobility so that everyone can have greater success, a better life, and a fairer chance of full development as a human being.

This last part of the book sets out three scenarios relating to social mobility. It asks policymakers and all of us to beware of false promises and easy solutions that proponents of greater social mobility can be tempted to offer. It calls for deeper changes in our societies and educational systems instead—changes that are mindful of the state of declining social mobility today in a world of widening inequalities, and of how it is almost impossible to advance social mobility without enhancing economic equality as well. We need to listen to more voices from the common people below in order to develop better policies at the top.

In the reference room of my local public library, as I searched for a way to succeed in my university-entrance history examination, second time around, it was not the views of history from the top that inspired me—whether these were about kings and queens, admirals and generals, or prime ministers and presidents. Rather, it was the history of so-called common, working people that sparked my curiosity—the history of people who invented and innovated, laboured and toiled, preached and educated, and took the world through great revolutions of agriculture and industry, creating whole towns and cities, like the one that raised me, as they did so.

Almost a half century later, I sat beside my mother's bed in the local community hospital, created from local workers' donations at the end of the 19th century, and had days to reflect on the life she had led—a life of being a weaver, a cleaner, a shop assistant, a child-minder, a mother, a neighbour, and a carer for my grandma too. It became clear to me that not only had her own life been worth living but also her life and the lives of women and men like her from working-class communities everywhere were worth writing about. It is now journalists, politicians, sports stars, entertainers, and business entrepreneurs, not monarchs and military leaders, who write personal histories that will be read in the future. So we must work extra hard, once more, to ensure that the lives of people from ordinary families and not just the rich and famous also get a telling and a hearing so that they become part of and help shape our sense of history and our future too.

This history from the bottom up is not just a commentary on everyday life. It also offers a view of what systems of power, politics, and privilege look like from underneath. Social mobility demands a lot of those who are experiencing it—ambition, resilience, ingenuity, perseverance, grit, and much more besides. But *the system* and those who are in charge of it also have a collective responsibility to go about the business of social and geographic mobility differently. Social mobility is too important to be left to individual effort, ingenuity, luck, or chance. Systems and governments must play their part as well.

This chapter therefore sketches out three contrasting and even competing scenarios for the future of social mobility and examines their implications for everyone.

1. Meritocracy
2. New aristocracy
3. Economic democracy

Meritocracy

Suppose there *was* perfect social mobility and everyone ended up exactly where they deserved to be, based completely on their achievement, effort, and merit. What would happen then? Surely this is what social-mobility advocates everywhere would want. Everyone would succeed according to his or her talent and ability. School mission statements all over the world stating that every student will fulfil his or her potential would no longer be just an aspiration, a wish, or a cliché. Now they would actually come true. And if there was perfect mobility in each generation and elites did not perpetuate themselves and become entrenched, perhaps all the angst and condescension would disappear as well.

This is the premise of a book written in 1958 by a British social reformer, Michael Young.[200] Young, who later became the aristocratically titled Lord Young of Dartington (a private, progressive school that he attended as a boy), popularized a little-known concept of Napoleon Bonaparte's—*méritocratie*. Despite his military triumphs, Napoleon was just a minor nobleman in the French aristocracy. With his heavy Corsican accent, he often suffered insults and slights about his inferior bloodline from his snobbish superiors. "Always alone among men," he wrote, "I come home to dream by myself and give myself over to all the forces of my melancholy."[201]

So after assuming military leadership, Napoleon was very motivated to make it payback time for the French upper class. Realistically, though, there were also many vacancies at the top of the military. After all, the French Revolution had already deposed, disposed of, and sometimes even decapitated its aristocracy. The vacancies had to be filled from somewhere. So Napoleon promoted his soldiers according to bravery and intelligence rather than their birthright.

Following Napoleon's lead, in *The Rise of the Meritocracy*, Michael Young imagines a society that would be governed "by the cleverest people; not an aristocracy of birth, not a plutocracy of wealth, but a true meritocracy of talent."[202] His thesis is not a piece of advocacy, though, but a satire. Excellence, Young argues with droll irony, is not distributed equally. "For every man enlivened by excellence, ten are deadened by mediocrity."[203] The mediocre individuals who have been protected by privilege, Young asserts, would no longer prevail in a meritocracy. The rise of talent from wherever it could be found would take over instead.

With more precise and accurate measurement tools, talent would be selected and developed earlier and earlier. Selective grammar schools would outlast all-inclusive comprehensive schools. Testing would be preferred over the subjective teacher assessments that had previously favoured children of the privileged who reminded teachers of their younger selves. And any late bloomers could be identified in later life so that further education could be provided for them to enable them to catch up.

Yet once everyone was where he or she deserved to be, what then? Well, Young speculates, some members of the meritocracy might become "so impressed with their own importance" they would "lose sympathy with the people whom they govern."[204] Meanwhile, because everyone gets a fair chance and can be tested, and tested again, those at the bottom might feel the "helpless despair" of their own inferiority, lose their self-respect, and consequently become neither good technicians nor good citizens.[205]

But the threat of resentment and rebellion could be staved off, Young says. Organized labour would lose its leadership once talent had been promoted out of it, so uprisings would be less probable. Frustrated parents could still hold out hopes for the fair chance that their children would have, and they might be prepared to wait a generation for those rewards. Meanwhile, the lower classes would be shielded from disappointment by their own stupidity. "They are unambitious, innocent, and incapable of grasping clearly enough the grand design of modern society to offer any effective protest," Young predicts.[206] Taking all the talent out of the lowest classes might consign them to inarticulate acceptance of their own diminished but transparently deserved fate.

So this was it, then. No longer would we ever have a Britain ruled by old Etonians and inheritors of privilege, like Prime Minister Boris de Pfeffel Johnson, while the disillusioned masses beneath in the forgotten industrial towns of the North bay for Brexit!

What are we to make of Young's fable? Some leaders have ignored or misunderstood Young's satirical intent and taken his ideas at face value. U.K. prime ministers Tony Blair and Theresa May both promoted meritocracy as a policy and a value.[207] Lee Kuan Yew, Singapore's founder, was an even more passionate advocate of meritocracy.[208] He vowed to transform his newly established nation from a Third World society to a globally competitive economy in just over a generation—and achieved immense success in doing so. Coming from a relatively modest background, but with a Cambridge University education behind him, Lee Kuan Yew advanced educational and social reform involving meritocracy. In the words of Professor Pak Tee Ng, Singapore's own leading interpreter of its educational system, Prime Minister Yew established "a highly competitive education system culminating in government scholarships, top positions in the civil service and political leadership . . . filled by individuals with demonstrated track records of merit as measured by achievements."[209]

Prime Minister Yew set out to offset the risks in *The Rise of the Meritocracy* by providing universal access to health care, affordable housing, and a strong school system that would develop a nation led by three hundred extremely talented people who would in turn promote, by merit, more talented people behind them.[210] Unlike the United States and even the United Kingdom, lack of educational or occupational success doesn't bring with it the spectre of social and economic insecurity, so dissatisfactions are less likely to surface. More than this, when Singapore teachers discuss their career paths on an annual basis with their superiors, exceptionally good ones are sometimes asked to transfer to schools where many students are struggling. Teachers regard these assignments as a great professional and national honour.[211]

But even when a meritocracy is initially successful, once it is in place, its beneficiaries begin to buy advantage for their own offspring. In Young's dark denouement, wealthy parents capitalize on advances in earlier and earlier testing to purchase smart infants from the lower classes beneath them. In England and the United States, wealthy parents already seek out homes in upmarket areas nearer higher-performing schools with better-paid teachers and leaders. And in Singapore, as in other parts of East Asia, more recent declines in social mobility have resulted from a vast system of private tutoring for test preparation and cram sessions after school that better-off parents can afford.[212]

In *Social Mobility: And Its Enemies*, Professor Lee Elliot Major, former executive director of the U.K. Sutton Trust (which is dedicated to improving social mobility), and economics professor Stephen Machin point out that the same trends are now emerging in Britain where a growth in private tuition by one-third between 2005 and 2016 has fuelled an "educational arms race" amongst parents.[213] Those who benefitted from equal opportunities as children now purchase unequal opportunities for children of their own.

And those of us who have been socially mobile, parents and grandparents alike, are all in it together. We want the best for our children, of course—extra classes, more desirable neighbourhoods, funds towards studying at better universities, or a foot in the door for internships with colleagues or friends—but this all comes at the cost of those who don't have those added educational experiences, high-end schools, or old-school-tie alumni. Writing in the *Atlantic* in 2018, Matthew Stewart describes these beneficiaries of the old meritocracy as the *new aristocracy*. "The meritocratic class," he argues, "has mastered the old trick of consolidating wealth and passing privilege along at the expense of other people's children."[214]

For all these reasons, meritocracy of talent combined with stark inequities of economic reward eventually start to put a brake on the escalator of educational and social advancement. And it takes little more than a generation to happen. The prospects and pathways for meritocracy and for the social mobility that results from it are now precarious at best. The old meritocracy becomes a new aristocracy. What does this new aristocracy actually look like, and is it inevitable?

New Aristocracy

One thing worse than the estrangement and resentment that is sometimes incurred by social mobility is the *absence* of social mobility. From the 1950s and 1960s through to the start of the Reagan and Thatcher years, there was what statisticians and social scientists called *net upward mobility*.[215] The economy expanded and grew. Investment in public life, including education, created new jobs. The rise of the consumer society produced growth in the service sector. And more women moved into the full-time-work economy, especially once they gained control over their reproductive choices. People moved up without others having to fall back. Mobility was not a zero-sum game.

However, in the leading Western economies, things changed dramatically for those born in and after the 1970s. Mobility slowed, came to a stop, and even went into reverse. In its 2018 report *A Broken Social Elevator? How to Promote Social Mobility*, the Organisation for Economic Co-operation and Development noted how:

> *Families and communities in many countries seem to be trapped on the bottom rungs of the social ladder, particularly since the early 1980s. This means that children born into the bottom of the income distribution have less chance to move up and improve their occupational status and earnings than their parents and previous generations.*[216]

Commenting on the report, the U.K. *Guardian* newspaper observed that "while income mobility was a reality for many people born between 1955 and 1975 from low-educated parents, it has stagnated for those born after the mid-1970s."[217] The *Wall Street Journal* reported similar findings as they applied to the United States.[218]

The combination of income inequality and social immobility is a toxic mix. Increasing concentrations of wealth amongst rich and influential elites reduce economic opportunity amongst those beneath them rather than providing trickle-down benefits. In 2016, professor of economics Emmanuel Saez and his colleagues showed that:

> *From 1980 to 2014, average national income per adult grew by 61 percent in the United States, yet the average pre-tax income of the bottom 50 percent of individual income earners stagnated at about $16,000 per adult after adjusting for inflation. In contrast, income skyrocketed at the top of the income distribution, rising 121 percent for the top 10 percent, 205 percent for the top 1 percent, and 636 percent for the top 0.001 percent.*[219]

In 1980, the richest 1 per cent of Americans earned twenty-seven times more than the lower 50 per cent. Now they earn more than eighty times more.[220] And these are the riches of those who are retiring on their capital, hiding their money in tax havens, and passing on their wealth to their heirs instead of creating jobs or paying taxes that would support public housing, public schools, and the overall public good that give others opportunities to step up towards a better life. The new aristocracy doesn't only protect and perpetuate educational and economic advantages for its own children; it also stockpiles its own wealth.

These levels of increasing inequality are not peculiar to the United States. The richest 1 per cent of people in the world own 48 per cent of the global wealth, with the remaining 52 per cent of this wealth being owned by the top 20 per cent of the rest of the population.[221] Severe inequalities are systematically associated with negative social and health outcomes, such as drug abuse and other addictions, teenage pregnancy, child obesity, and educational underachievement.[222]

In late 2018, the United Nations (UN) poverty envoy, Philip Alston, wrote a scathing indictment of how U.K. austerity policies had increased poverty in ways that were "punitive, mean-spirited, and often callous," leaving one-fifth of the U.K. population in poverty, with the numbers rising.[223] Alston's 2018 report pointed to calamitous policies in the United Kingdom, such as cutting the funding to local authorities and their services by half, restricting child benefit to the first two children only, and instituting measures that made claiming financial benefits a long and drawn-out process that pushed many families into destitution and meant that vulnerable claimants "struggled to survive."[224]

All this is portrayed in director Ken Loach's heartbreaking movie *I, Daniel Blake*, about a working-class man plunged into a bureaucratic abyss of repeatedly failed attempts to claim benefits after a heart attack. After the welfare-benefits system treats him with institutionalized indifference and casual contempt, Loach's protagonist defiantly proclaims:

> *My name is Daniel Blake.*
>
> *I am a man, not a dog.*
>
> *As such, I demand my rights.*
>
> *I demand you treat me with respect.*
>
> *I, Daniel Blake, am a citizen, nothing more and nothing less.*[225]

The highest and lowest echelons of society are becoming more and more insulated from each other as subsidies are slashed at the bottom and as reduced inheritance taxes, along with unpaid internships covered by privileged parents at the top, widen the gap, or the distance that those seeking mobility must travel. In *Social Mobility: And Its Enemies*, Lee Elliot Major and Stephen Machin observe that "the rich have been pulling away from the poorer people behind them" so that "it is harder for people to catch up."[226] The rungs on the ladder of mobility are getting further and further apart.

Since the 2007 global economic collapse, in southern Europe, economic austerity policies have pushed youth unemployment to astronomical levels. They still stand around 30 per cent in Spain, Italy, and Greece.[227] In the United Kingdom and the United States, meanwhile, university and college fees have continued to rise along with associated levels of student debt. The result is that young people from families with fewer resources tend to live at home and go to lower-status institutions that offer poorer prospects for social mobility than more traditional universities.

Meanwhile the artificial intelligence (AI) revolution is eliminating jobs in all kinds of occupations, from call centres to supermarket checkouts and even teaching and lecturing, as online courses and adjunct professors replace tenured or career faculty with digital alternatives.[228] And, as I mentioned before, once the competition heats up, those who have the privilege, connections, and resources protect themselves and one another by acquiring tutors, purchasing second properties in the neighbourhoods of high-performing schools, angling for internships for their youngsters, and even getting fraudulent placements or athletics scholarships for their children at high-status universities in return for donations and bribes.[229]

By inhibiting social mobility and opportunity, these high levels of increasing inequality destroy hope. They also inflame feelings of resentment. In *Poverty Safari*, Darren McGarvey, a survivor of chronic deprivation in the United Kingdom, is not the least bit surprised that the poor who eke out an existence on Glasgow's council estates didn't shed any tears when the Glasgow School of Art burned down—or that they despise immigrants and are strong supporters of

Brexit, even though very few of them ever actually vote. Their decaying community centres, with their broken equipment and dilapidated buildings, seem to communicate only abandonment by their government. Meanwhile, McGarvey is incensed that the liberal Left that once supported their working-class struggle is now wrapped up in the identity politics of recognizing the *intersectionalities* of every other marginalized group—refugees; women; gay, lesbian, and transgender individuals; and so on—everyone other than working-class boys and men like him who, he protests, are unreasonably supposed to check their "privilege" as straight white males despite upbringings riddled with poverty, drugs, alcoholism, homelessness, and abuse.[230]

Prize-winning sociologist Arlie Russell Hochschild went to live amongst families in the heavily polluted bayous of Louisiana to understand their conservative loyalties and their associated sense of resentment. In *Strangers in Their Own Land*, she explains how these hardworking conservative families who have been robbed of their fish, family members, and livelihoods by unregulated toxic dumping from the petrochemical industry tend to compare themselves with those who have a bit more affluence or advantage than they have, rather than with those who have lifestyles that seem beyond reach.[231]

Why do they do this? Back in 1966, British professor W. G. Runciman came up with the concept and book title of *Relative Deprivation and Social Justice* to describe how people tend to identify with those who have just a little more wealth and status than they've got, rather than with those whose lifestyles appear to be marked by great opulence.[232] This is one aspect of what Sigmund Freud called the "narcissism of minor differences."[233] Instead of being outraged about corporate greed and irresponsibility, those who struggle to make a living direct their anger against those who, in their eyes, are creating the problems by cutting in line just ahead of them: immigrants who *undercut their wages*, welfare *scroungers* who consume public revenue, and the bureaucrats of *big government* and *fat cats* of teachers' unions with their generous pensions and other *undeserved* benefits.

So although social mobility can bring problems as well as benefits, having new aristocracies that perpetuate lack of social mobility in the profoundly unequal kind of societies in which many people now live is not an acceptable alternative. It produces a vast range of social problems and fans the flames of resentment against and violence towards outsiders who seem to threaten people's livelihoods and ways of life.

One answer to this new aristocracy that is the end point of the inherent flaws of meritocracy, therefore, may be found not in trying to improve meritocracy but in reducing the economic inequality that drives people to protect their own privilege in the first place. Let's consider this prospect in more detail.

Economic Democracy

When Pitirim Sorokin introduced the idea of vertical mobility, what he had in mind was two kinds of things that could move up or down. One sort of vertical mobility occurred when people moved between layers as individuals, gaining or losing money or status over the course of their lives and in relation to their parents. This is how most of us typically think about social mobility. But there is also a second kind of movement, according to Sorokin. This involves shifts in the positions of entire groups or classes so that the social strata themselves move closer together or further apart, in terms of the size of the income gaps between them, for example.

This is the kind of social mobility that concerns bestselling authors Richard Wilkinson and Kate Pickett. Wilkinson and Pickett have become the global gurus of economic inequality and its pervasive consequences for society. In *The Spirit Level*, they bring together a wealth of global data to show that increases in economic inequality create greater ill-being and suffering in society in terms of violence, bullying, mental illness, obesity, educational underachievement, substance abuse, and many other problematic aspects of social life.[234] The sequel, *The Inner Level*, which draws on an extensive review of additional research, spells out what the chief problem is. It's not destitution, they say. It's status.[235]

The more economic inequality there is, the more people worry about how they stack up in relation to others and about the threat of falling behind, of sliding down the social ladder. The problems, say Wilkinson and Pickett, "are driven by the stress of social status differences themselves, stresses which get worse the lower you are on the social ladder and the bigger the status differences."[236] It's not just how low you can go that's the issue; it's how far away you are from everyone else, including the people nearest to you, that is critical too. Social-status issues and all their consequences get worse "when bigger income differences make the status differences larger and more important."[237]

Not surprisingly, therefore, "more unequal countries have less social mobility."[238] In countries with great income disparities, like the United Kingdom and the United States, children from poor or even modest-income families have far fewer opportunities than those in countries with smaller disparities. More equal countries, such as those in Scandinavia, have around half the income-inequality gaps of countries like the United Kingdom and the United States—and their social, psychological, and educational problems are much smaller.

The answer to this toxic relationship between economic inequality, low mobility, and a range of other social problems, say Wilkinson and Pickett, is what they call *economic democracy*.[239] Economic democracy is about redistributing income and wealth more fairly on a national and a global scale. It is about bringing social strata closer together by ending corporate tax havens, increasing corporate taxes and wealth taxes, and restricting the ability of large multinationals to avoid paying taxes in the countries where they trade by moving their corporate headquarters elsewhere. And there is no good reason why the differentials between CEOs and frontline workers should be tenfold what they were forty years ago, in the executive *bonus culture* of the 21st century.[240]

Economic democracy is also about allocating greater attention, priority, and resources to publicly or cooperatively run institutions. The democratic nature of these institutions introduces greater economic fairness in salaries and rewards for employees of different ranks and abilities. The disparities are consistently smaller than they are in the private sector, so a stronger and larger public sector reduces economic disparities and improves social mobility overall. In addition to creating greater equality, employee involvement in company ownership and management also increases innovation and long-term sustainability, they say. And, as I mentioned earlier, the economic democracy of a strong public sector offers fairer opportunities and more transparent pathways to advancement for the upwardly mobile too.[241]

The Future

What are the implications for social and economic reform in favour of greater equality? How exactly might smaller status differences in society reduce the intensity of the need for social mobility and also improve mobility rates in society? How can greater equality lead to more mobility? And in the meantime, what can educational institutions do to improve all young people's opportunities and experiences? This memoir, and the implications arising from it, now ends with practical steps that can and should be taken to move the equity and mobility agenda forward in society and education.

Government Policy

Individuals and institutions cannot combat inequality or enhance opportunity all by themselves. The great majority of the differences in educational achievement that are related to family background are explained by poverty and other social factors. Only about 20 per cent, on average, are attributable to the school.[242] So the greatest levers for improving equality and social mobility are to be found in society and especially in social policy. Here are five things in social policy that can make a big difference to levels of equity and rates of social mobility.

First, stop accepting and promoting extreme economic inequality.

Not only does the increasing individualism and growing resentment that accompany it reduce people's chances of mobility. It makes their experience of it more and more difficult as the rungs on the ladder get further apart and the people climbing up together shrink in number. Change is possible. Canada, for example, has far lower economic inequality than the United States and the United Kingdom and also double their rates of social mobility.[243] Scandinavia and northern Europe are not the only exceptions to extreme inequality. I grew up and went to school in the golden era of social mobility in the 1960s and 1970s, when economic disparities were much smaller—and the opportunities for mobility were much greater—than they are today. It was hard enough for me and others like me when the whole system was skewed a bit more in our favour. Imagine what it's like now that the system is tilted the other way.

Second, restore a strong social state and public sector.

Social mobility depends to some extent on individual qualities like resilience. Indeed, my favourite karaoke choice is from a one-hit-wonder band, Chumbawamba, who hail from near my hometown. Their song "Tubthumping," about individual resilience and working-class resistance, has the chorus "I get knocked down, but I get up again. You're never gonna keep me down."[244] My friends and associates tell me that, as a rule, I'm pretty good at bouncing back from adversity. *Stubborn* is another word for it. In 2019, just over six months after I'd had surgery on the double break on my ankle that I had sustained while hiking an isolated section of the U.S. Appalachian Trail, I was back up there again, walking up to sixteen miles and climbing thousands of feet a day over the rocky ridges of Pennsylvania and the mountains of Maine.

But all the resilience I might have had in the world as a child and a teenager would have come to nothing without a strong social state. Public investment provided us with welfare benefits when my mum could no longer cope, with a public library where I could read and study, and with enough financial support for higher education so I could go away from home, to the university I wanted, without having to work in the evenings or at the weekends to support myself. Some have said this is no longer practical, but in northern Europe, especially, where taxes are higher and the social state is stronger, it remains commonplace. And even in the United States and United Kingdom, where university tuition rates have risen the fastest, free or significantly reduced tuition costs are at the forefront of election manifestos once again.

Reinvesting in public education, of course, also means turning away from market solutions to school improvement, like charter schools in the United States, academies in England, and free schools in Sweden. These have been associated with deliberate disinvestment in local communities and redirection of previous public investment towards private profit. Reinvestment means returning to supporting and developing state schools in their local districts and communities so that everyone's best school will also be his or her nearest school. This is what bestselling author Pasi Sahlberg says is already the case in his own country of Finland, which has excelled for almost two decades on international achievement tests.[245]

Prominent education critic and former U.S. assistant secretary of education Diane Ravitch, in her 2020 book *Slaying Goliath: The Passionate Resistance to Privatization and the Fight to Save America's Public Schools*, summarizes the copious evidence on the relative effectiveness of charter schools compared to traditional local district schools. Charter schools, she concludes, have demonstrated no overall superiority compared to their public-school equivalents.[246] After more than a decade of disruption and distraction, they have also yielded no national improvement in measured achievement or equity for U.S. children. They have done nothing to narrow achievement gaps or improve social mobility. The only yield, she says, has been a lucrative financial one for these schools' multimillion-dollar owners and suppliers.

Across the Atlantic, a key study by economists Helen Ladd and Edward Fiske of differences in performance between England's quasi-private academies and the local authority or district schools they replaced also shows that there have been no educational benefits for students as a result of this profound and disruptive system-wide change.[247] Academies, charter schools, and free schools have been driven by individual competitive achievement, choice, and financial gain, not commitment to the common public good that has been the historic foundation of public education.

Ideologies of markets and austerity have cut back the public sector in many countries, weakened trades unions, and outsourced jobs to private contract. Yet a strong public sector is a feature of nations like Finland and Canada, where high educational performance and social mobility are especially robust. A strong public sector of jobs in education, health, public administration, and social services is also a career route for the upwardly mobile that does not depend so much on their having networks and inside contacts in order to get a start in adult life. And it is a place of mission, purpose, and service—the very thing many young people now say they have been missing—where upwardly mobile teachers, public servants, and health workers can give something back to the communities and societies that raised them.

Third, refrain from forcing immigrants and class migrants to give up one identity in order to have another.

A lot of social mobility involves geographic mobility as well—whether this is from the other side of the tracks or the far side of the world. Moving countries entails at least as much disruption as moving classes. Immigrants should not be made to feel that they have to abandon what they were in order to become fully British, American, or German, for example, but that they can proudly be like how many Canadians feel they are: half-Canadian—whether that's Japanese Canadian, Jamaican Canadian, or whatever. Bilingualism should be treated as an asset, not a deficit. Having two cultures should be regarded as an addition, not a subtraction.

In his 2018 book, *Identity: The Demand for Dignity and the Politics of Resentment*, Stanford University professor Francis Fukuyama insists that everyone should have only one passport, to set aside ambiguity about how they identify and where they belong.[248] By contrast, in her 2015 book, *Teaching Transnational Youth: Literacy and Education in a Changing World*, University of Texas–Austin professor Allison Skerrett sets out her research findings that show many immigrant families are actually transnational—simultaneously retaining family connections and obligations in their original home countries and in their new host countries—and she argues that they should be supported in managing those relationships.[249] We shouldn't force people who migrate between countries to choose between the future and the past—to give up their language, abandon their values, or hide their traditional cultural pastimes—and we shouldn't expect people who migrate between social classes to do so either.

Fourth, include the working class in definitions and discussions of diversity.

The working class, some of which is white working class in the countries where I have lived and worked, is part of diversity, not an exception to it. Whatever its history and legacy, it must be given a name and a voice like all other cultures and communities. If it is not acknowledged, known, and treated with dignity, its members will become resentful of others' opportunities for education and social mobility. The white working class will have less mobility rather than more and will turn against others who, they feel, seek and gain advancement at their expense.[250]

The area where I grew up has been one of the biggest strongholds for Brexit. While governments have invested money for urban and cultural renewal in London's East End and Manchester city centre, the businesses, schools, and neighbourhoods of former mill towns like mine, or declining coastal towns like Blackpool where my grandmother grew up and where eight out of ten of the poorest neighbourhoods in Britain are now located, have been overlooked and left far behind.[251] If liberal democratic and socialist parties continue to pitch their appeal to the middle class, to urban and financial cosmopolitans, and to a rainbow coalition of historically disenfranchised minorities alone, then the white working class will increasingly turn aside from the narrative of democracy and mobility and embrace the evils of demagoguery instead. In this respect, after U.S. Democrats had spent years avoiding mentioning the working class and referring to them euphemistically as "the middle class" instead, it is a heartening glimmer of hope to hear and read Michelle Obama speak proudly and openly of working-class values and her own working-class upbringing, helping this aspect of her own and other's identities to come out into the open.[252]

Last, make internships illegal—unless they are supplied through accredited career and vocational programmes in schools, colleges, or other training and retraining organizations.

A 2017 review of employment contracts urged the U.K. government to ensure that "exploitative unpaid internships which damage social mobility in the UK are stamped out."[253] But the government's acceptance of this recommendation has been weakly enforced at best. Unpaid and unaccredited internships are doubly egregious. They provide privileged families with inside connections to high-status organizations and with job experiences that give their own children preferential advantages in establishing middle-class careers. They also supply the private sector with free labour that erodes opportunities for legitimate job seekers. An accredited, transparent system for organizing internships will increase the likelihood that high-status opportunities can be accessed by everyone, irrespective of economic circumstances or family background.

Educational Institutions

As society changes, and governments alter their approach to equity and social mobility, those who work in schools and universities and whose credentials and credentialing processes profoundly affect everyone's opportunities cannot sit back and wait for all the necessary transformations to occur elsewhere. Poverty and economic inequality may still be the major impediments to social mobility, but the way we organize our educational institutions and systems matters as well. So what positive and concrete steps can educators take to enhance social mobility?

First, give students from poor postcodes extra credit when they apply for university, a scholarship, or some other cherished opportunity.

To get high grades, high U.S. SAT scores, or good examination results, wherever you go to school, is admirable. To get the same grades in a challenging school or community where very few others do so is extraordinary. We already know that students from state schools do better, grade for grade, when they get to university compared to their privately educated counterparts.[254] So, as some universities have already tried to do—though not without pushback from the privileged—we should also regard a slightly lower score from a high-poverty school as being equivalent to a higher score from a more privileged one. If students can do really well when the winds are against them, imagine what they could achieve with the wind at their backs.

Second, overlook and overcome social awkwardness amongst people with great talents.

When young people from poorer backgrounds are being interviewed or taking their first stab at leadership, they may not possess all the finesse of their more privileged peers. But a diffident start or fumbling beginning shouldn't get in the way of our capacity to identify or enhance their gifts. When I was interviewed for an associate professorship at the Ontario Institute for Studies in Education in Toronto in the mid-1980s when I was still in my thirties, one letter of reference warned the selection committee that I was "raw. And I mean raw!" But the letter went on to say I had other important talents that outweighed my ineptitude in the social niceties of academic life and that were worth investing in. If people commit a faux pas or fail at something the first time round because they are all at sea in an unfamiliar culture, we should help them get better at it next time, rather than hastily write them off as being unfit for the college or the job.

Third, rethink what a strong CV looks like.

The leadership opportunities we expect candidates to take on often presuppose a level of income, privilege, or surplus time that might allow them to volunteer, travel, work as an unpaid intern, or take up an extra hobby or two. For young people from poor families, leadership may instead show up in taking on part-time work, caring for sick parents or younger siblings, overcoming a significant disability, and so on. We should find a way for young people in challenging circumstances to be proud rather than ashamed of these experiences, and to provide exemplars and opportunities—another box on the application form or an item in a submitted portfolio, perhaps—where they can give voice to them.

Fourth, ensure that students' learning is engaging and often connects with their lives.

Redefining cultural capital means redefining what counts as worthwhile knowledge. *All* students—not just those in private schools, wealthy suburbs, or higher streams or tracks—should be able to work on engaging projects that connect with and also reach beyond who they are, just like in Mary Hindle's class. It's important to make the curriculum engaging for everyone. But it's especially important for students who live in challenging circumstances, where, in order to succeed, they must surmount massive distractions and disruptions like poverty, violence, prejudice, sleeplessness, posttraumatic stress, and other family and community issues. The curriculum for students in schools that serve poorer communities shouldn't be reduced to preparing for standardized tests and reaching minimal proficiency in basic skills. Nor should young people be confronted only with remote historical figures or abstruse literary texts that are alien to their own experience. Young people shouldn't have to set their interests and their lives aside in order to succeed.

Equity isn't just about equalizing test scores or narrowing achievement gaps in literacy and mathematics. It is about getting all students to succeed, whatever their backgrounds, by making them feel and be included in their schools, their curricula, and their learning.

Last, broaden what counts as cultural capital, in speech, habits, knowledge, and taste.

When I moved to the United States in 2002, I became part of a nation that imagines itself to be far less preoccupied with class or status than the United Kingdom. So I was astonished to discover how selection discussions, academic conversations, dinner parties, and conference receptions were permeated with downright snooty distinctions about which "school," meaning university, people had gone to—Harvard or Yale, cloistered liberal-arts college or state university, and so on. In more egalitarian Canada, or Scandinavia, by contrast, these comparisons are practically meaningless, as private or ultraelite universities are almost nonexistent. It mainly matters only whether you went to university and how well you did, not which one you attended. Social mobility demands not only new behaviours from those who aspire to reach the top but also less condescending or self-important ones from those who are already there.

This applies in schools as well. Uniforms, prize-giving ceremonies, trophy cabinets, selection criteria for student leadership roles, the content of extracurricular activities, the social mix in a school, and the tendency to conflate elite ethnocultural diversity (which happens in most elite private schools now) with social-class equality of opportunity—all these aspects of school culture, within and beyond the curriculum, should be reviewed to make schools as inclusive and welcoming as possible.

Last Words

Social mobility is about families who seek better lives for their children. It is often about one generation sacrificing for another. It is also about young people deferring immediate gratification for longer-term reward. Social mobility needs grit, determination, and resiliency in the struggle to succeed. It often needs ingenuity and stubborn defiance to work around and against the system as well.

The socially mobile also need parents who will support them and teachers who will stand by them. They need schools and universities that understand the struggles they have in their lives and that provide interventions and supports to help them cope. They need an engaging curriculum and inspired teaching so that achievement rests on more than stoic endurance—or, in Charles Dickens's words, being "severely workful" about memorizing esoteric content or taking interminable tests.[255]

A socially mobile life should be a world of *both–and*, not *either–or*. It should allow people to have more than one passport. People's pasts should not be held hostage to their futures. We need a world where high culture and popular culture can coexist, where Karl Marx and the Dixie Chicks can belong on the same page, side by side. Social mobility should enable people to find success without losing themselves. And a more equitable society with smaller gaps, where whole groups and not just individuals move closer to one another, should make all these movements more usual and less stressful.

Moving on up will always have those complications that Curtis Mayfield warned us about.[256] But a decent society with a socially just state that brings people closer together will make the complications more manageable. Whenever I faced a test or a challenge, my mum's simple advice was always "Just do your best, lad. You can't do any more than that." That's what we must now ask of our leaders in governments, business, and education. It's time for all of us to do our very best, to reduce inequality, increase support, and foster more inclusive and responsive cultures in our schools, our universities, and our societies. If we do all this, social mobility will become a stronger possibility for more young people and a less alienating experience once they achieve it.

Notes

Acknowledgments

1. Ainscow, M. (2015). *Towards self-improving school systems: Lessons from a city challenge.* London: Routledge.

2. The original article is to be found in Johnson, G. (2013, December 11). How a loving Accrington mum scrimped and worked for her family. *The Lancashire Telegraph.* Accessed at www.lancashiretelegraph.co.uk/news/10870126.how-a-loving-accrington-mum-scrimped-and-worked-for-her-family/ on October 1, 2019.

3. Hargreaves, A. (2004). Distinction and disgust: The emotional politics of school failure. *International Journal of Leadership in Education, 7*(1), 27–41.

Preface

4. Sorokin, Pitirim Aleksandrovich. (n.d.). Accessed at www.encyclopedia.com/environment/encyclopedias-almanacs-transcripts-and-maps/sorokin-pitirim-aleksandrovich on December 19, 2019.

5. Sorokin, P. A. (1959). *Social and cultural mobility.* Glencoe, IL: Free Press, p. 133. (Original work published 1927).

Chapter 1

6. Mayfield, C. (1970). Move on up. On *Curtis* [CD]. Chicago: RCA Studios.

7. Graham, A. D., Coleman, M., & Shebib, N. (2013). Started from the bottom [Recorded by A. D. Graham]. On *Nothing was the same* [CD]. New Orleans, LA: Cash Money Records.

8. Hanley, L. (2016). *Respectable: The experience of class.* London: Allen Lane.

9. Reay, D. (2017). *Miseducation: Inequality, education, and the working classes.* Bristol, England: Policy Press.

10. Winterson, J. (2011). *Why be happy when you could be normal?* London: Jonathan Cape.

11. McGarvey, D. (2017). *Poverty safari: Understanding the anger of Britain's underclass.* London: Picador.

12. Vance, J. D. (2016). *Hillbilly elegy: A memoir of a family and culture in crisis.* New York: HarperCollins.

13. Westover, T. (2018). *Educated: A memoir.* New York: Random House.

14. Hoggart, R. (1957). *The uses of literacy.* London: Chatto and Windus.

15. Bannatyne, D. (2007). *Anyone can do it: My story.* London: Orion.

16. Major, L. E., & Machin, S. (2018). *Social mobility: And its enemies.* London: Pelican.

17. McCourt, F. (1996). *Angela's ashes: A memoir.* New York: Scribner.

18. The 4 Yorkshiremen. (n.d.). Accessed at www.montypython.net/scripts/4york.php on October 1, 2019.

19. BBC News. (2012, February 23). *Frank Carson: It's the way he told 'em* [Video file]. Accessed at www.bbc.co.uk/news/uk-northern-ireland-17142351 on October 1, 2019.

20. Johnson, G. (2013, December 11). How a loving Accrington mum scrimped and worked for her family. *The Lancashire Telegraph.* Accessed at www.lancashiretelegraph.co.uk/news/10870126.how-a-loving-accrington-mum-scrimped-and-worked-for-her-family/ on October 1, 2019.

21. Johnson, G. (2013, December 11). How a loving Accrington mum scrimped and worked for her family. *The Lancashire Telegraph.* Accessed at www.lancashiretelegraph.co.uk/news/10870126.how-a-loving-accrington-mum-scrimped-and-worked-for-her-family/ on October 1, 2019.

22. Johnson, G. (2013, December 11). How a loving Accrington mum scrimped and worked for her family. *The Lancashire Telegraph.* Accessed at www.lancashiretelegraph.co.uk/news/10870126.how-a-loving-accrington-mum-scrimped-and-worked-for-her-family/ on October 1, 2019.

23. "I Have a Dream," address delivered at the March on Washington for Jobs and Freedom. (n.d.). *Stanford: The Martin Luther King, Jr. Research and Education Institute.* Accessed at https://kinginstitute.stanford.edu/king-papers/documents/i-have-dream-address-delivered-march-washington-

jobs-and-freedom on January 22, 2020.

24. Cavani, E. (2018, June 29). Letter to my younger self. *The Players' Tribune.* Accessed at www.theplayerstribune.com/en-us/articles/edinson-cavani-uruguay-letter-to-my-younger-self on October 1, 2019.

25. Cavani, E. (2018, June 29). Letter to my younger self. *The Players' Tribune.* Accessed at www.theplayerstribune.com/en-us/articles/edinson-cavani-uruguay-letter-to-my-younger-self on October 1, 2019.

26. Cavani, E. (2018, June 29). Letter to my younger self. *The Players' Tribune.* Accessed at www.theplayerstribune.com/en-us/articles/edinson-cavani-uruguay-letter-to-my-younger-self on October 1, 2019.

27. Duckworth, A. (2016). *Grit: The power of passion and perseverance.* New York: Scribner.

28. Ackerley, T. (Producer), Robbie, M. (Producer), Rogers, S. (Producer), Unkeless, B. (Producer), & Gillespie, C. (Director). (2017). *I, Tonya* [Motion picture]. Los Angeles: LuckyChap Entertainment.

Chapter 2

29. Johnson, G. (2013, December 11). How a loving Accrington mum scrimped and worked for her family. *The Lancashire Telegraph.* Accessed at www.lancashiretelegraph.co.uk/news/10870126.how-a-loving-accrington-mum-scrimped-and-worked-for-her-family/ on October 1, 2019.

30. Johnson, G. (2013, December 11). How a loving Accrington mum scrimped and worked for her family. *The Lancashire Telegraph.* Accessed at www.lancashiretelegraph.co.uk/news/10870126.how-a-loving-accrington-mum-scrimped-and-worked-for-her-family/ on October 1, 2019.

31. Johnson, G. (2013, December 11). How a loving Accrington mum scrimped and worked for her family. *The Lancashire Telegraph.* Accessed at www.lancashiretelegraph.co.uk/news/10870126.how-a-loving-accrington-mum-scrimped-and-worked-for-her-family/ on October 1, 2019.

32. Johnson, G. (2013, December 11). How a loving Accrington mum scrimped and worked for her family. *The Lancashire Telegraph.* Accessed at www.lancashiretelegraph.co.uk/news/10870126.how-a-loving-accrington-mum-scrimped-and-worked-for-her-family/ on October 1, 2019.

33. Johnson, G. (2013, December 11). How a loving Accrington mum scrimped and worked for her family. *The Lancashire Telegraph.* Accessed at www.lancashiretelegraph.co.uk/news/10870126.how-a-loving-accrington

-mum-scrimped-and-worked-for-her-family/ on October 1, 2019.

34. Morrison, M. (2015, April 21). Under-fire Liverpool boss Brendan Rodgers has rundown Accrington terrace conviction overturned. *The Lancashire Telegraph.* Accessed at www.lancashiretelegraph.co.uk/news/12901657.under-fire-liverpool-boss-brendan-rodgers-has-rundown-accrington-terrace-conviction-overturned/ on October 2, 2019.

35. Woodruff, W. (1993). *The road to Nab End.* London: Little, Brown Book Group.

36. Johnson, G. (2013, December 11). How a loving Accrington mum scrimped and worked for her family. *The Lancashire Telegraph.* Accessed at www.lancashiretelegraph.co.uk/news/10870126.how-a-loving-accrington-mum-scrimped-and-worked-for-her-family/ on October 1, 2019. For more information on Britain's postwar welfare state, see Hanley, L. (2012). *Estates: An intimate history.* London: Granta Books.

37. Johnson, G. (2013, December 11). How a loving Accrington mum scrimped and worked for her family. *The Lancashire Telegraph.* Accessed at www.lancashiretelegraph.co.uk/news/10870126.how-a-loving-accrington-mum-scrimped-and-worked-for-her-family/ on October 1, 2019.

38. Workshop of the world. (n.d.). Accessed at www.encyclopedia.com/humanities/dictionaries-thesauruses-pictures-and-press-releases/workshop-world on December 18, 2019.

39. Wyatt, L. T. (2009). *The Industrial Revolution.* Westport, CT: Greenwood Press.

40. Winterson, J. (2011). *Why be happy when you could be normal?* London: Jonathan Cape.

41. vinnielo1. (2007, February 16). *Ian Rush, Accrington Stanley milk advert, clean and in full!* [Video file]. Accessed at www.youtube.com/watch?v=pieK7b4KLL4 on October 2, 2019. The TV ad was first shown in 1988. Originally, the derogatory reference was meant to be to Tottenham Hotspur, but after they objected, Accrington Stanley, then an obscure nonleague team, known to have fallen on hard times, was selected instead.

42. Chrysanthou, A. (2018, December 6). Are you living in any of England's top ten worst towns? Surprising list revealed. *Express.* Accessed at www.express.co.uk/news/uk/1055269/England-worst-town-list-huddersfield-rotherham on September 30, 2019.

43. Brown, P. (2018, May 23). World Cup 1966: They think it's all over. *Medium.* Accessed at https://medium.com/@paulbrownUK/world-cup-1966-they-think-its-all-over-3810879df5fe on October 9, 2019.

Kenneth Wolstenholme was the TV commentator for the 1966 World Cup between England and West Germany that England won 4–2. After a see-saw game, England took the lead 3–2, and as Wolstenholme noticed celebrating fans coming onto the pitch—and then saw England score one more goal as they did so—he uttered the now legendary quote "They think it's all over. It is now."

44. Shindler, N. (Executive producer), Wainwright, S. (Executive producer), Sherry, T. (Executive producer), & Jones, S. (Executive producer). (2011–2016). *Scott and Bailey* [Television series]. London: Red Production Company.

45. From the archive, 22 January 1964: Colour bar at working men's club remains. (2014, January 22). *The Guardian.* Accessed at www.theguardian.com/theguardian/the-northerner/2014/jan/22/racism-race-bar-working-men-accrington on December 18, 2019.

46. Hargreaves, A., Boyle, A., & Harris, A. (2014). *Uplifting leadership: How organizations, teams, and communities raise performance.* San Francisco: Jossey-Bass.

47. Blakemore, N. [BBC Newsnight]. (2016, June 24). *Burnley and Brexit: "We've done it!"—BBC Newsnight* [Video file]. Accessed at www.youtube.com/watch?v=Oq3qdX2TGps on October 2, 2019.

48. Chibnall, C. (Executive producer), Strevens, M. (Executive producer), & Hoyle, S. (Executive producer). (2018). *Doctor Who* [Television series]. London: BBC.

49. Eccleston, C. (2019). *I love the bones of you: My father and the making of me.* London: Simon & Schuster.

50. Jones, O. (2011). *Chavs: The demonization of the working class.* London: Verso.

51. Dickens, C. (1995). *Hard times.* London: Penguin, pp. 28–29. (Original work published 1854).

52. Orwell, G. (1937). *The road to Wigan Pier.* London: Victor Gollancz.

53. Ricks, T. (2017). *Churchill and Orwell: The fight for freedom.* New York: Penguin.

54. Bourdieu, P. (1984). *Distinction: A social critique of the judgement of taste.* Cambridge, MA: Harvard University Press. Hargreaves, A. (2004). Distinction and disgust: The emotional politics of school failure. *International Journal of Leadership in Education, 7*(1), 27–41.

55. Smith, A. (1853). *The theory of moral sentiments* (Revised ed.). London: Henry. G. Bohn, p. 20.

56. Miller, W. I. (1997). *The anatomy of disgust.* Cambridge, MA: Harvard University Press.

57. Darwin, C. (1872). *The expression of the emotions in man and animals.* London: John Murray, p. 254.

58. Darwin, C. (1872). *The expression of the emotions in man and animals.* London: John Murray, p. 257.

59. See Hargreaves, A. (2004). Distinction and disgust: The emotional politics of school failure. *International Journal of Leadership in Education, 7*(1), 27–41.

60. Darwin, C. (1872). *The expression of the emotions in man and animals.* London: John Murray, p. 256.

61. Hargreaves, A. (2004). Distinction and disgust: The emotional politics of school failure. *International Journal of Leadership in Education, 7*(1), 27–41.

62. Hargreaves, A. (2004). Distinction and disgust: The emotional politics of school failure. *International Journal of Leadership in Education, 7*(1), 27–41.

63. Ryan, J., & Sackrey, C. (1984). *Strangers in paradise: Academics from the working class.* Boston: South End Press.

64. Hargreaves, A. (2004). Distinction and disgust: The emotional politics of school failure. *International Journal of Leadership in Education, 7*(1), 27–41.

65. Chrysanthou, A. (2018, December 6). Are you living in any of England's top ten worst towns? Surprising list revealed. *Express.* Accessed at www.express.co.uk/news/uk/1055269/England-worst-town-list-huddersfield-rotherham on September 30, 2019.

66. Fullan, M. (2018). *Surreal change: The real life of transforming public education.* New York: Routledge.

67. Beatles. (2000). *The Beatles anthology.* San Francisco: Chronicle Books, p. 158.

68. Everly, D., & Everly, P. (1966). The price of love [Recorded by the Everly Brothers]. On *In our image* [CD]. Los Angeles: Warner Brothers.

Chapter 3

69. Stevenson, A., & Waite, M. (Eds.). (2011). *Concise Oxford English dictionary* (12th ed.). New York: Oxford University Press, p. 1081.

70. These terms were first defined and established by Victorian economic and social reformer Alfred Marshall. See Marshall, A. (1925). The future of the working classes. In A. C. Pigou (Ed.), *Memorials of Alfred Marshall* (pp. 101–118). London: MacMillan. (Original work published 1873).

71. Bambrough, R. (1963). *The philosophy of Aristotle.* New York: Signet Books.

72. Douglas, J. W. B. (1964). *The home and the school.* London: MacGibbon & Kee.

73. Jackson, B. (1964). *Streaming: An education system in miniature.* London: Routledge & Kegan Paul.

74. Hargreaves, A., & Earl, L. (1990). *Rights of passage: A review of selected research about schooling in the transition years.* Toronto: Queen's Printer for Ontario.

75. Douglas, J. W. B. (1964). *The home and the school.* London: MacGibbon & Kee.

76. The *Seven Up!* documentary first aired on U.K. Granada Television in 1964, and subsequent episodes in the *Up* series were broadcast on ITV Granada every seven years through *63 Up* in 2019—except for the sixth episode, which was broadcast on BBC. The director of *Seven Up!* was Paul Almond, and all subsequent documentaries were directed by Michael Apted.

77. Granger, D. (Executive producer), Hewat, T. (Executive producer), & Almond, P. (Director). (1964). *Seven up!* [Television documentary]. London: ITV.

78. Organisation for Economic Co-operation and Development. (2013). *PISA 2012 results: What makes schools successful: Resources, policies and practices (volume iv).* Paris: Author.

79. Marshall, A. (1925). The future of the working classes. In A. C. Pigou (Ed.), *Memorials of Alfred Marshall* (pp. 101–118). London: MacMillan. (Original work published 1873).

80. A great and lasting bone of contention between my mum and dad was that a workmate of my dad's successfully pressured him to split his winnings with him, on the grounds that he had given my dad the competition entry form.

81. Selected excerpts from the inspection report were shared with me by the governors of Spring Hill Community Primary School as part of a collection of archival records from the school that they felt would be of interest to me.

82. Ofsted. (2001, June). *Spring Hill Primary School, Accrington, Inspection Report* (Reference Number 119185). Accessed at https://files.api.ofsted.gov.uk/v1/file/779299 on October 2, 2019.

83. Ofsted. (2001, June). *Spring Hill Primary School, Accrington, Inspection Report* (Reference Number 119185). Accessed at https://files.api.ofsted.gov.uk/v1/file/779299 on October 2, 2019.

84. This quotation from Mary Hindle was included in Spring Hill Community School. (2004, May 6). *Odd notes from childhood: Compiled for Professor Andy Hargreaves on the occasion of his unveiling of the new school foundation stone*, p. 6. The original material was submitted by the late Mary Hindle in longhand to the school for its centennial in 1999. Many thanks to former head teacher Stephanie Grimshaw for locating this material.

85. See Donnachie, I. (2005). *Robert Owen: Social visionary* (2nd ed.). Edinburgh: John Donald. Simon, B. (1981). *The two nations and the educational structure, 1780–1870* (Vol. 1). London: Lawrence & Wishart.

86. This quotation from Mary Hindle was also included in Spring Hill Community School. (2004, May 6). *Odd notes from childhood: Compiled for Professor Andy Hargreaves on the occasion of his unveiling of the new school foundation stone*, p. 6.

87. "Malagueña" was first recorded on *Lecuona Plays Lecuona*, a 1955 RCA Victor LP. It was adapted for flamenco guitar by Carlos Montoya in 1961, on another RCA Victor live album by the artist—1961 being just one year before we heard and danced to it in our music-and-movement classes.

88. See, for example, Silberman, C. (1970). *Crisis in the classroom: The remaking of American education.* New York: Random House.

89. Central Advisory Council for Education. (1967). *Children and their primary schools (the Plowden report)* (Vol. 1). London: HMSO.

90. Central Advisory Council for Education. (1967). *Children and their primary schools (the Plowden report)* (Vol. 1). London: HMSO, p. 185.

91. Central Advisory Council for Education. (1967). *Children and their primary schools (the Plowden report)* (Vol. 1). London: HMSO, p. 187.

92. See Sahlberg, P. (2011). The fourth way of Finland. *Journal of Educational Change, 12*(2), 173–185. Ravitch, D. (2011). *The death and life of the great American school system: How testing and choice are undermining education.* New York: Basic Books. Zhao, Y. (2018). *What works may hurt: Side effects in education.* New York: Teachers College Press. Seligman, M. E. P. (2011). *Flourish: A visionary new understanding of happiness and well-being.* New York: Free Press. Hargreaves, A., & Shirley, D. (2018, November 29). Well-being and success: Opposites that need to attract. *EdCan Network.* Accessed at www.edcan.ca/articles/well-being-and-success/ on October 2, 2019.

93. Thich Nhat Hanh. (2011). *Your true home: The everyday wisdom of Thich Nhat Hanh.* Boston: Shambhala.

94. Storr, W. (2017). *Selfie: How we became so self-obsessed and what it's doing to us.* London: Picador.

95. The beginning of this backlash against progressivism was, in political terms, expressed in Cox, C. B., & Dyson, A. E. (Eds.). (1971). *The black papers on education.* London: Davis-Poynter Ltd. In research terms, the first major study claiming that there were either no effects or only negative effects of progressive strategies was Bennett, N. (1976). *Teaching styles and pupil progress.* London: Open Books. In the United States, the educational backlash began with the National Commission on Excellence in Education. (1983). *A nation at risk: The imperative for educational reform.* Washington, DC: U.S. Government Printing Office.

96. Dewey, J. (1916). *Democracy and education.* New York: MacMillan.

97. Central Advisory Council for Education. (1967). *Children and their primary schools (the Plowden report)* (Vol. 1). London: HMSO, p. 188.

98. Robinson, K. (2009). *The element: How finding your passion changes everything.* New York: Viking.

99. Hallowell, E. M., & Ratey, J. J. (1994). *Driven to distraction: Recognizing and coping with attention deficit disorder from childhood to adulthood.* New York: Pantheon Books.

100. Tedx Talks. (2016, July 13). *Uplifting your performance, your people and yourself | Andy Hargreaves | TEDxUnisinos* [Video file]. Accessed at www.youtube.com/watch?v=Ao9mwfGvm-o on October 28, 2019.

101. Cook, C. (2004, May 7). Clapper happy: Ex-pupil unveils new building. *Lancashire Evening Telegraph.*

102. Cohen, L. (1992). Anthem. On *The future* [CD]. New York: Columbia Records. "Anthem" by Leonard Cohen. Copyright © 1992 by Leonard Cohen, used by permission of The Wylie Agency LLC.

Chapter 4

103. Lee, M., & Larson, R. (2000, April). The Korean "examination hell": Long hours of studying, distress, and depression. *Journal of Youth and Adolescence, 29*(2), 249–271.

104. See Zhao, Y. (2018). *What works may hurt: Side effects in education.* New York: Teachers College Press.

105. Bray, M. (2006). Private supplementary tutoring: Comparative perspectives on patterns and implications. *Compare, 36*(4), 515–530.

106. Organisation for Economic Co-operation and Development. (2017). *PISA 2015 results (volume iii): Students' well-being.* Paris: Author.
107. See Reay, D. (2017). *Miseducation: Inequality, education, and the working classes.* Bristol, England: Policy Press.
108. See Ravitch, D. (2011). *The death and life of the great American school system: How testing and choice are undermining education.* New York: Basic Books. Ravitch, D. (2020). *Slaying Goliath: The passionate resistance to privatization and the fight to save America's public schools.* New York: Knopf. Zhao, Y. (2018). *What works may hurt: Side effects in education.* New York: Teachers College Press.
109. Campbell, C., Clinton, J., Fullan, M., Hargreaves, A., James, C., & Longboat, K. D. (2018, March). *Ontario: A learning province.* Toronto: Queen's Printer for Ontario.
110. Committee of the Secondary School Examinations Council. (1943). *Curriculum and examinations in secondary schools (the Norwood report).* London: HMSO.
111. Committee of the Secondary School Examinations Council. (1943). *Curriculum and examinations in secondary schools (the Norwood report).* London: HMSO, p. 2.
112. Committee of the Secondary School Examinations Council. (1943). *Curriculum and examinations in secondary schools (the Norwood report).* London: HMSO, p. 2.
113. Committee of the Secondary School Examinations Council. (1943). *Curriculum and examinations in secondary schools (the Norwood report).* London: HMSO, p. 3.
114. Committee of the Secondary School Examinations Council. (1943). *Curriculum and examinations in secondary schools (the Norwood report).* London: HMSO, p. 3.
115. Committee of the Secondary School Examinations Council. (1943). *Curriculum and examinations in secondary schools (the Norwood report).* London: HMSO, p. 4.
116. Committee of the Secondary School Examinations Council. (1943). *Curriculum and examinations in secondary schools (the Norwood report).* London: HMSO, p. 4.
117. Committee of the Secondary School Examinations Council. (1943). *Curriculum and examinations in secondary schools (the Norwood report).* London: HMSO, p. 4.

118. BBC News. (2016, September 9). *Grammar schools: May's vision of a "great meritocracy"* [Video file]. Accessed at www.bbc.co.uk/news/av/uk-37322955/grammar-schools-may-s-vision-of-a-great-meritocracy on December 18, 2019.

119. Sutton Trust. (2013, November). *Sutton Trust: Prep schools provide four times more grammar school entrants than FSM pupils.* Accessed at www.suttontrust.com/newsarchive/sutton-trust-prep-schools-provide-four-times-grammar-school-entrants-fsm-pupils/ on December 18, 2019.

120. Cribb, J., Jesson, D., Sibieta, L., Skipp, A., & Vignoles, A. (2013, November). *Poor grammar: Entry into grammar schools for disadvantaged pupils in England.* London: Sutton Trust, p. 5.

121. Drabble, M. (1987). *The radiant way.* London: Weidenfeld & Nicolson.

122. Duckworth, A. (2016). *Grit: The power of passion and perseverance.* New York: Scribner.

123. Snow, C. P. (1993). *The two cultures.* London: Cambridge University Press.

124. Thomas, D. (2015, February 12). *Diary 30—as rare as Suet Sprinkles.* Accessed at https://m.thefootballnetwork.net/main/burnley/s37/st188449/diary-30—as-rare-as-suet-sprinkles on October 8, 2019.

125. Dweck, C. S. (2006). *Mindset: The new psychology of success.* New York: Random House.

126. Putnam, R. D. (2015). *Our kids: The American Dream in crisis.* New York: Simon & Schuster. Harris, A., Muijs, D., Chapman, C., Stoll, L., & Russ, J. (2003). *Raising attainment in schools in former coalfield areas* (Research report 423). London: Department for Education and Skills.

127. Douglas, J. W. B., Ross, J. M., & Simpson, H. R. (1971). *All our future: A longitudinal study of secondary education.* London: Panther, p. 38.

128. Sutton Trust. (2015, June). *Research brief: Missing talent* (5th ed.). Accessed at www.suttontrust.com/wp-content/uploads/2015/06/Missing-Talent-final-june-1.pdf on October 2, 2019.

129. Putnam, R. D. (2015). *Our kids: The American Dream in crisis.* New York: Simon & Schuster.

130. See Krulwich, R. (2013, October 16). Successful children who lost a parent—why are there so many of them? *National Public Radio.* Accessed at www.npr.org/sections/krulwich/2013/10/15/234737083/successful-children-who-lost-a-parent-why-are-there-so-many-of-them on October 2, 2019. Gladwell, M. (2008). *Outliers: The story of success.* New York: Little, Brown. Eisenstadt, M., Haynal, A., Rentchnick, P., & de Senarclens, P. (1989). *Parental loss and achievement.* Madison, CT: International Universities Press.

131. Cicourel, A. V., & Kitsuse, J. I. (1963). *The educational decision-makers.* Indianapolis: Bobbs-Merrill.

132. Best, R. E., Jarvis, C. B., & Ribbins, P. M. (1977). Pastoral care: Concept and process. *British Journal of Educational Studies, 25*(2), 124–135. Lang, P. (1984). Pastoral care: Some reflections on possible influences. *Pastoral Care in Education, 2*(2), 136–146. Power, S. (1996). *The pastoral and the academic.* London: Cassell.

133. Shaw, L. (2006, November 5). Foundation's small-schools experiment has yet to yield big results. *The Seattle Times.* Accessed at www.seattletimes.com/seattle-news/foundations-small-schools-experiment-has-yet-to-yield-big-results/ on December 18, 2019.

134. Reviews of Bosworth Academy from the Whole Education Network can be found at Whole Education Peer Review. (n.d.). Accessed at www.bosworthacademy.org.uk/parents/whole-education-peer-review/ on December 19, 2019.

135. Walsh, M. E., Madaus, G. F., Raczek, A. E., Dearing, E., Foley, C., An, C., et al. (2014, August). A new model for student support in high-poverty urban elementary schools: Effects on elementary and middle school academic outcomes. *American Educational Research Journal, 51*(4), 704–737. Accessed at https://doi.org/10.3102/0002831214541669 on October 8, 2019.

136. Walsh, M. E., Madaus, G. F., Raczek, A. E., Dearing, E., Foley, C., An, C., et al. (2014, August). A new model for student support in high-poverty urban elementary schools: Effects on elementary and middle school academic outcomes. *American Educational Research Journal, 51*(4), 704–737. Accessed at https://doi.org/10.3102/0002831214541669 on October 8, 2019.

137. Hargreaves, A., Earl, L., & Ryan, J. (1996). *Schooling for change.* London: Falmer Press.

138. The key research is reviewed and referenced in ASCD. (2012). *Making the case for educating the whole child.* Alexandria, VA: Author. Accessed at www.wholechildeducation.org/assets/content/mx-resources/WholeChild-MakingTheCase.pdf on December 19, 2019.

Chapter 5

139. Chrysanthou, A. (2018, December 6). Are you living in any of England's top ten worst towns? Surprising list revealed. *Express.* Accessed at www.express.co.uk/news/uk/1055269/England-worst-town-list-huddersfield-rotherham on September 30, 2019.

140. Jackson, B., & Marsden, D. (1966). *Education and the working class.* London: Penguin.

141. McCulloch, G. (1994). *Educational reconstruction: The 1944 Education Act and the twenty-first century.* Ilford, England: Woburn Press.

142. Gramsci, A. (1971). *Selections from the prison notebooks.* Q. Hoare & G. N. Smith (Eds.). London: Lawrence & Wishart.

143. Jackson, B., & Marsden, D. (1966). *Education and the working class.* London: Penguin.

144. Jackson, B., & Marsden, D. (1966). *Education and the working class.* London: Penguin, p. 68.

145. Jackson, B., & Marsden, D. (1966). *Education and the working class.* London: Penguin, p. 70.

146. Jackson, B., & Marsden, D. (1966). *Education and the working class.* London: Penguin, p. 70.

147. See Mills, C. W. (1951). *White collar: The American middle classes.* New York: Oxford University Press.

148. Coe, J. (2001). *The Rotters' club.* London: Viking.

149. Wainwright, A. (1968). *Pennine Way companion.* Kendal, England: Westmorland Gazette.

150. Jackson, B., & Marsden, D. (1966). *Education and the working class.* London: Penguin, p. 110.

151. Jackson, B., & Marsden, D. (1966). *Education and the working class.* London: Penguin, p. 122.

152. Committee of the Secondary School Examinations Council. (1943). *Curriculum and examinations in secondary schools (the Norwood report).* London: HMSO, p. 2.

153. Bourdieu, P., & Passeron, J. C. (1977). *Reproduction in education, society and culture.* London: Sage Publications.

154. Eccleston, C. (2019). *I love the bones of you: My father and the making of me.* London: Simon & Schuster.

155. Lawrence, D. H. (1913). *Sons and lovers.* London: Gerald Duckworth & Co.

156. Storey, D. (1976). *Saville.* London: Jonathan Cape, p. 158.

157. Storey, D. (1976). *Saville.* London: Jonathan Cape, p. 462.

158. Storey, D. (1976). *Saville.* London: Jonathan Cape, p. 462.

159. Noah, T. (2016). *Born a crime.* New York: Spiegel & Grau.

160. Noah, T. (2016). *Born a crime.* New York: Spiegel & Grau, p. 57.

161. Noah, T. (2016). *Born a crime.* New York: Spiegel & Grau, p. 141.

162. Vance, J. D. (2016). *Hillbilly elegy: A memoir of a family and culture in crisis.* New York: HarperCollins.

163. Vance, J. D. (2016). *Hillbilly elegy: A memoir of a family and culture in crisis.* New York: HarperCollins, p. 50.

164. Vance, J. D. (2016). *Hillbilly elegy: A memoir of a family and culture in crisis.* New York: HarperCollins, p. 41.

165. Vance, J. D. (2016). *Hillbilly elegy: A memoir of a family and culture in crisis.* New York: HarperCollins, p. 139.

166. Marshall, A. (1925). The future of the working classes. In A. C. Pigou (Ed.), *Memorials of Alfred Marshall* (pp. 101–118). London: MacMillan. (Original work published 1873).

167. Vance, J. D. (2016). *Hillbilly elegy: A memoir of a family and culture in crisis.* New York: HarperCollins, p. 149.

168. Vance, J. D. (2016). *Hillbilly elegy: A memoir of a family and culture in crisis.* New York: HarperCollins, p. 146.

169. Carmon, I., & Knizhnik, S. (2015). *Notorious RBG: The life and times of Ruth Bader Ginsburg.* New York: HarperCollins.

170. Said, E. (2000). *Out of place: A memoir.* New York: Vintage Books.

Chapter 6

171. morpheusatloppers. (2009, November 15). *Monty Python: The parrot sketch & the lumberjack song movie versions HQ* [Video file]. Accessed at www.youtube.com/watch?v=vnciwwsvNcc on October 7, 2019. The Spanish Inquisition sketch. (n.d.). Accessed at www.montypython.net/scripts/spanish.php on December 6, 2019. The argument sketch. (n.d.). Accessed at www.montypython.net/scripts/argument.php on December 6, 2019.

172. Lodge, D. (1980). *How far can you go?* London: Secker & Warburg.

173. Stevens, C. (1970). Hard headed woman. On *Tea for the tillerman* [CD]. London: Island.

174. Comte, A. (1835). *Cours de Philosophie Positive* (Vol. 2). Paris: Bachelier. Accessed at www.gutenberg.org/files/31882/31882-h/31882-h.htm on December 19, 2019.

175. Symbolic interactionism (SI) is a theory of how human selves, identities, and cultures are formed through interactions with others and how they reflect our selves back to us. Much of this work evolved in Chicago. It began with Charles H. Cooley's 1902 depiction of the "looking glass self," where others serve as a mirror for the development of our own identities. See Cooley, C. H. (1902). *Human nature and the social order.* New York: Scribner. The foundational theorist of SI was arguably George Herbert Mead (1934), who distinguished between the *I* (rather like Freud's *ego* and *id*) and the social *me* that was built through other people's perceptions of and feedback to us. See Mead, G. H. (1934). *Mind, self and society.* Chicago: University of Chicago Press. W. I. Thomas and D. S. Thomas (1928) memorably added to this body of work the claim that situations defined as real are real in their consequences—it's the collective perception of reality that ultimately counts. See Thomas, W. I., & Thomas, D. S. (1928). *The child in America.* New York: Knopf. Over time, a lot of this work in what became known as the Chicago School of Sociology focused on the cultures, careers, and identities that people developed in different occupations and forms of work, including teaching, which in many ways set the course of my own research on cultures of teaching and professional collaboration. See Hargreaves, A. (1994). *Changing teachers, changing times: Teachers' work and culture in the postmodern age.* London: Cassell. But when I was an undergraduate, it was another sociologist of the 1960s—the Canadian Erving Goffman—who caught my attention. Goffman described how people's selves in everyday life were deliberate and variable constructions. See Goffman, E. (1959). *The presentation of self in everyday life.* New York: Doubleday. Undertaking fieldwork in a Scottish mental institution, he noted how asylums were a kind of total institution, like the army, or boarding schools, that stripped people of their identities to furnish them with new ones that fit the convenience and purpose of these institutions. See Goffman, E. (1961). *Asylums: Essays on the social situation of mental patients and other inmates.* New York: Anchor Books. He also developed a theory of stigma and stigmatization about identities that are marginalized or ignored that, in my own work, remains highly relevant to my research on the development of identity through education today. See Goffman, E. (1963). *Stigma: Notes on the management of spoiled identity.* Englewood Cliffs, NJ: Prentice-Hall.

176. Postman, N., & Weingartner, C. (1969). *Teaching as a subversive activity.* New York: Delacorte Press.

177. Kozol, J. (1968). *Death at an early age.* London: Penguin.

178. Freire, P. (1970). *Pedagogy of the oppressed.* London: Penguin.

179. Illich, I. (1971). *Deschooling society.* New York: Harper & Row.

180. Holt, J. (1969). *How children fail.* London: Penguin, p. 9.

181. Holt, J. (1969). *How children fail.* London: Penguin, p. 95.

182. Holt, J. (1969). *How children fail.* London: Penguin, p. 95.

183. Holt, J. (1969). *How children fail.* London: Penguin, p. 95.

184. Holt, J. (1969). *How children fail.* London: Penguin, p. 28.

185. Holt, J. (1969). *How children fail.* London: Penguin, p. 25.

186. Holt, J. (1969). *How children fail.* London: Penguin, p. 29.

187. Holt, J. (1969). *How children fail.* London: Penguin, p. 59.

188. Holt, J. (1969). *How children fail.* London: Penguin, p. 77.

189. Holt, J. (1969). *How children fail.* London: Penguin, p. 149.

190. See Hargreaves, A. (in press). Large-scale assessments and their effects: The case of midstakes tests in Ontario. *Journal of Educational Change.*

191. Detailed tables of unemployment for this period can be found in Denman, J., & McDonald, P. (1996). Unemployment statistics from 1881 to the present day. *Labour Market Trends*, 5–18.

Chapter 7

192. Pasolini, U. (Producer), & Cattaneo, P. (Director). (1997). *The full monty* [Motion picture]. Century City, CA: Fox Searchlight Pictures.

193. Full monty. (n.d.). In *Cambridge Dictionary.* Accessed at https://dictionary.cambridge.org/dictionary/english/full-monty on September 30, 2019.

194. Shaw, G. B. (2006). *Man and superman.* Teddington, England: Echo Library.

195. Lacey, C. (1977). *The socialization of teachers.* London: Methuen.

196. Chrysanthou, A. (2018, December 6). Are you living in any of England's top ten worst towns? Surprising list revealed. *Express.* Accessed at www.express.co.uk/news/uk/1055269/England-worst-town-list-huddersfield-rotherham on September 30, 2019.

197. Freire, P. (1970). *Pedagogy of the oppressed.* London: Penguin.

198. Booth, R. (2019, February 4). Anxiety on rise among the young in social media age. *The Guardian.* Accessed at www.theguardian.com/society/2019/feb/05/youth-unhappiness-uk-doubles-in-past-10-years on September 30, 2019.

199. Springer, M. A. (1992). Two sparrows in a hurricane [Recorded by T. Tucker]. On *Can't run from yourself* [CD]. Nashville: Liberty.

Chapter 8

200. Young, M. (1961). *The rise of the meritocracy, 1870–2033.* London: Penguin.

201. Seeley, M. (2011, March–April). The weight of change: Meritocracy and nepotism within Napoleonic Europe. *The Napoleonic Historical Society Newsletter.* Accessed at http://napoleonsightings.blogspot.com/2011/05/napoleonic-nepotism-and-meritocracy.html on October 2, 2019.

202. Young, M. (1961). *The rise of the meritocracy, 1870–2033.* London: Penguin, p. 21.

203. Young, M. (1961). *The rise of the meritocracy, 1870–2033.* London: Penguin, p. 40.

204. Young, M. (1961). *The rise of the meritocracy, 1870–2033.* London: Penguin, p. 107.

205. Young, M. (1961). *The rise of the meritocracy, 1870–2033.* London: Penguin, p. 124.

206. Young, M. (1961). *The rise of the meritocracy, 1870–2033.* London: Penguin, p. 111.

207. Read Civil, D. (2017, June 26). *May's "meritocracy" might be on hold, but the ideas behind it are here to stay.* Accessed at https://theconversation.com/mays-meritocracy-might-be-on-hold-but-the-ideas-behind-it-are-here-to-stay-79967 on December 18, 2019.

208. Kwang, H. F., Ibrahim, Z., Hoong, C. M., Lim, L., Low, I., Lin, R., et al. (2011). *Lee Kuan Yew: Hard truths to keep Singapore going.* Singapore: Straits Times Press.

209. Ng, P. T. (2017). *Learning from Singapore: The power of paradoxes.* New York: Routledge, p. 61.

210. Kwang, H. F., Ibrahim, Z., Hoong, C. M., Lim, L., Low, I., Lin, R., et al. (2011). *Lee Kuan Yew: Hard truths to keep Singapore going.* Singapore: Straits Times Press.

211. See Organisation for Economic Co-operation and Development. (2011). *Strong performers and successful reformers in education: Lessons from PISA for the United States.* Paris: Author. Tucker, M. (2019). *Leading high-performance school systems: Lessons from the world's best.* Alexandria, VA: ASCD. Hargreaves, A., & Shirley, D. (2012). *The global fourth way: The quest for educational excellence.* Thousand Oaks, CA: Corwin.

212. See Ng, P. T. (2017). *Learning from Singapore: The power of paradoxes.* New York: Routledge. Bray, M. (2006). Private supplementary tutoring: Comparative perspectives on patterns and implications. *Compare, 36* (4), 515–530.

213. Major, L. E., & Machin, S. (2018). *Social mobility: And its enemies.* London: Pelican, p. 81.

214. Stewart, M. (2018, June). The 9.9 percent is the new American aristocracy. *The Atlantic.* Accessed at www.theatlantic.com/magazine/archive/2018/06/the-birth-of-a-new-american-aristocracy/559130/ on October 2, 2019.

215. Goldthorpe, J. H., & Mills, C. (2004). Trends in intergenerational class mobility in Britain in the late twentieth century. In R. Breen (Ed.), *Social mobility in Europe* (pp. 195–224). Oxford: Oxford University Press.

216. Organisation for Economic Co-operation and Development. (2018). *A broken social elevator? How to promote social mobility.* Paris: Author. Accessed at www.oecd.org/social/soc/Social-mobility-2018-Overview-MainFindings.pdf on October 1, 2019.

217. Inman, P. (2018, June 15). Social mobility in richest countries "has stalled since 1990s." *The Guardian.* Accessed at www.theguardian.com/society/2018/jun/15/social-mobility-in-richest-countries-has-stalled-since-1990s on October 1, 2019.

218. Hannon, P. (2018, June 15). OECD sounds alarm over "broken elevator" for social mobility. *The Wall Street Journal.* Accessed at www.wsj.com/articles/oecd-sounds-alarm-over-broken-elevator-for-social-mobility-1529053726 on October 1, 2019.

219. Saez, E., Piketty, T., & Zucman, G. (2016, December 6). Economic growth in the United States: A tale of two countries. *The Washington Center for Equitable Growth.* Accessed at https://equitablegrowth.org/economic-growth-in-the-united-states-a-tale-of-two-countries/ on October 1, 2019.

220. Saez, E., Piketty, T., & Zucman, G. (2016, December 6). Economic growth in the United States: A tale of two countries. *The Washington Center for Equitable Growth.* Accessed at https://equitablegrowth.org/economic-growth-in-the-united-states-a-tale-of-two-countries/ on October 1, 2019.

221. Oxfam. (2015, January). Wealth: Having it all and wanting more. *Oxfam Issue Briefing.* Accessed at https://www-cdn.oxfam.org/s3fs-public/file_attachments/ib-wealth-having-all-wanting-more-190115-en.pdf on October 1, 2019.

222. Wilkinson, R., & Pickett, K. (2010). *The spirit level: Why greater equality makes societies stronger.* New York: Bloomsbury Press.

223. Booth, R., & Butler, P. (2018, November 16). UK austerity has inflicted "great misery" on citizens, UN says. *The Guardian.* Accessed at www.theguardian.com/society/2018/nov/16/uk-austerity-has-inflicted-great-misery-on-citizens-un-says on October 1, 2019.

224. Booth, R., & Butler, P. (2018, November 16). UK austerity has inflicted "great misery" on citizens, UN says. *The Guardian.* Accessed at www.theguardian.com/society/2018/nov/16/uk-austerity-has-inflicted-great-misery-on-citizens-un-says on October 1, 2019.

225. O'Brien, R. (Producer), & Loach, K. (Director). (2016). *I, Daniel Blake* [Motion picture]. London: Sixteen Films.

226. Major, L. E., & Machin, S. (2018). *Social mobility: And its enemies.* London: Pelican, p. 16.

227. Eurostat. (2019, September 30). *Unemployment statistics.* Accessed at https://ec.europa.eu/eurostat/statistics-explained/index.php/Unemployment_statistics#Youth_unemployment on October 1, 2019.

228. Two different sides of the argument about the opportunities and drawbacks of artificial intelligence and its actual and potential impact can be found respectively in the following: Sahota, N., & Ashley, M. (2019). *Own the AI revolution: Unlock your artificial intelligence strategy to disrupt your competition.* New York: McGraw-Hill. Smith, G. (2018). *The AI delusion.* Oxford: Oxford University Press.

229. Baker, V. (2019, March 15). Celebrity parents and the bizarre "cheating" scandal. *BBC News.* Accessed at www.bbc.com/news/world-us-canada-47585336 on October 1, 2019.

230. McGarvey, D. (2017). *Poverty safari: Understanding the anger of Britain's underclass.* London: Picador.

231. Hochschild, A. R. (2016). *Strangers in their own land: Anger and mourning on the American right.* New York: New Press.

232. Runciman, W. G. (1966). *Relative deprivation and social justice.* London: Routledge & Kegan Paul.

233. Freud, S. (1930). *Civilization and its discontents.* London: Hogarth Press.

234. Wilkinson, R., & Pickett, K. (2010). *The spirit level: Why greater equality makes societies stronger.* New York: Bloomsbury Press.

235. Wilkinson, R., & Pickett, K. (2018). *The inner level: How more equal societies reduce stress, restore sanity and improve everyone's wellbeing.* London: Penguin Press.

236. Wilkinson, R., & Pickett, K. (2018). *The inner level: How more equal societies reduce stress, restore sanity and improve everyone's wellbeing.* London: Penguin Press, p. 3.

237. Wilkinson, R., & Pickett, K. (2018). *The inner level: How more equal societies reduce stress, restore sanity and improve everyone's wellbeing.* London: Penguin Press, pp. 4–5.

238. Wilkinson, R., & Pickett, K. (2018). *The inner level: How more equal societies reduce stress, restore sanity and improve everyone's wellbeing.* London: Penguin Press, p. 186.

239. Wilkinson, R., & Pickett, K. (2018). *The inner level: How more equal societies reduce stress, restore sanity and improve everyone's wellbeing.* London: Penguin Press.

240. Wilkinson, R., & Pickett, K. (2018). *The inner level: How more equal societies reduce stress, restore sanity and improve everyone's wellbeing.* London: Penguin Press.

241. Wilkinson, R., & Pickett, K. (2018). *The inner level: How more equal societies reduce stress, restore sanity and improve everyone's wellbeing.* London: Penguin Press.

242. Rothstein, R. (2004). *Class and schools: Using social, economic, and educational reform to close the black–white achievement gap.* Washington, DC: Economic Policy Institute. Ainscow, M., Dyson, A., Goldrick, S., & Kerr, K. (2008). *Equity in education: Responding to context.* Manchester: Centre for Equity in Education, University of Manchester. Berliner, D. C. (2006). Our impoverished view of educational reform. *Teachers College Record, 108*(6), 949–995.

243. Major, L. E., & Machin, S. (2018). *Social mobility: And its enemies.* London: Pelican.

244. Chumbawamba. (1997). Tubthumping. On *Tubthumper* [CD]. London: EMI.

245. Sahlberg, P. (2011). The fourth way of Finland. *Journal of Educational Change, 12*(2), 173–185.

246. Ravitch, D. (2020). *Slaying Goliath: The passionate resistance to privatization and the fight to save America's public schools.* New York: Knopf.

247. Ladd, H. F., & Fiske, E. B. (2016, October 25). *England confronts the limits of school autonomy* (National Center for the Study of Privatization in Education [NCSPE] Working paper 232). New York: Teachers College.

248. Fukuyama, F. (2018). *Identity: The demand for dignity and the politics of resentment.* New York: Farrar, Straus and Giroux.

249. Skerrett, A. (2015). *Teaching transnational youth: Literacy and education in a changing world.* New York: Teachers College Press.

250. For discussions about "white trash"—or, in British terms, working-class "chavs"—as an overlooked source and form of stigma, read the following: Isenberg, N. (2016). *White trash: The 400-year untold history of class in America.* New York: Penguin. Hochschild, A. R. (2016). *Strangers in their own land: Anger and mourning on the American right.* New York: New Press. Williams, J. C. (2017). *White working class: Overcoming class cluelessness in America.* Boston: Harvard Business Review Press. Jones, O. (2011). *Chavs: The demonization of the working class.* London: Verso.

251. BBC News. (2019, September 26). *England's most deprived areas named as Jaywick and Blackpool.* Accessed at www.bbc.com/news/uk-england-49812519 on December 18, 2019.

252. Obama, M. (2018). *Becoming.* New York: Crown.

253. Taylor, M., Marsh, G., Nicol, D., & Broadbent, P. (2017). *Good work: The Taylor review of modern working practices.* London: Department for Business, Energy & Industrial Strategy. Accessed at https://assets.publishing.service.gov.uk/government/uploads/system/uploads/attachment_data/file/627671/good-work-taylor-review-modern-working-practices-rg.pdf on December 19, 2019. Reported in BBC News. (2018, February 9). *Government steps up action on unpaid internships.* Accessed at www.bbc.com/news/business-42997400 on December 19, 2019.

254. Grove, J. (2014, March 28). *State pupils on same grades as private counterparts "get better degrees."* Accessed at www.timeshighereducation.com/news/state-pupils-on-same-grades-as-private-counterparts-get-better-degrees/2012325.article on December 18, 2019.

255. Dickens, C. (1854). *Hard times.* London: Bradbury and Evans, p. 29.

256. Mayfield, C. (1970). Move on up. On *Curtis* [CD]. Chicago: RCA Studios.

Praise for

Moving:

A Memoir of Education and Social Mobility

"A nuanced and heartfelt account of his early years by one of the leading educators of our time. One comes to appreciate the motivations for Andrew Hargreaves's lifetime mission of improving educational opportunities for less privileged persons, as well as the approaches that he has taken in pursuit of that essential undertaking."

—**Howard Gardner**
Hobbs Research Professor of Cognition and Education,
Harvard Graduate School of Education

"You will not read a more personal, passionate, and powerful account of social mobility. Hargreaves's moving life story offers universal lessons for us all."

—**Lee Elliot Major**
Professor of Social Mobility, University of Exeter

"Brilliant! Using humour, poignant storytelling, and scholarly argument, Andy Hargreaves presents us with his personal journey from humble roots as a young boy in northern England to his current status as a world-class educational leader in explaining the concept of *social mobility*. This book is a must-read for all individuals who want to understand the role of education in effecting social change such that there are reduced disparities in this world and greater equity and equality of opportunity for everyone. Everyone reading this book will see a part of themselves in Andy's story and reflect on the narrative to consider how they might ensure a better life for all."

—**Steve Cardwell**
President, Learning Forward

A Summing Up: Teaching and Learning in Effective Schools and PLCs at Work®
Robert Eaker
Learn from a master educator as he shares the story of his career, along with in-depth guidance for implementing the PLC at Work® process.
BKF943

Change Wars
Edited by Andy Hargreaves and Michael Fullan
What can organizations do to create profound, enduring changes? International experts prove successful change can be a realistic goal and then explore constructive alternatives to traditional change strategies.
BKF254

21st Century Skills: Rethinking How Students Learn
Edited by James A. Bellanca and Ron Brandt
Education luminaries reveal why 21st century skills are necessary, which skills are most important, and how to help schools include them in curriculum and instruction.
BKF389

Visit SolutionTree.com or call 800.733.6786 to order.